eating wildly

eating wildly

a personal animal food chain

CHRIS HEAL

Published by Chattaway and Spottiswood
Four Marks, Hampshire
www.candspublishing.org.uk

chrisheal@candspublishing.org.uk

All rights reserved. No part of this publication may be reproduced,
stored in a retrieval system or transmitted, in any form or by
any means, electronic, mechanical, photocopying, recording or
otherwise, without prior permission in writing from the publisher.

© Chris Heal, 2025

The moral right of Chris Heal to be identified as the author of this work has been asserted.

The names, characters and quotes of the principal characters, events and incidents are memories of the author, except where stated otherwise.
Opinions about events, characters and organisations are the views of the author.

A catalogue record for this book is available from
the British Library.

ISBN 978-1-9161944-6-5

Design and typeset: Mary Woolley, www.battlefield-design.co.uk
Cover, print and website: Andy Severn, www.oxford-ebooks.com
Printed on demand: www.ingramspark.com

for fellow animal eaters:
ailsa, charlie, emily, holly and murray

Contents

                      Page

introduction   11

out of africa   15
anchovy, catfish, frog, horse, monkey, nile perch, nile tilapia, sandre, snail (9)

crawly things   25
weaver ant larva, stink bug, house cricket, short-tailed cricket, grasshopper, wasp larva, palm weevil (7)

diving delights   31
barnacle, crawfish, conger eel, horse mussel, lobster, razor fish, scallop, queenie scallop, sea urchin (9)

the great elephant cull   39
elephant (1)

fish'n'chips'n'biafra   41
cod, coley, spiny dogfish, gurnard, haddock, hake, halibut, kingklip, lumpfish, pollock, snoek, sturgeon, tilapia, whiting (14)

flatfish by knife   47
dab, plaice, skate, turbot (4)

fresh water book party   53
signal crayfish, eider duck, pike, roach, tench (5)

fruits de mer & jellied eel — 59
clam, cockle, crab, spider crab, crevette, eel, krill, langoustine, mussel, oyster, periwinkle, prawn, shrimp, whelk (14)

garden fare — 65
crow, partridge, pheasant, quail, rabbit, red deer, squirrel, turkey, wood pigeon (9)

guga hunt — 71
gannet (1)

hippie trail — 77
chicken, cockroach, goat, sheep (4)

among the icebergs — 83
abalone, emperor penguin, seal, walrus, killer whale (5)

island love affairs — 89
armadillo, conch, kipper, mahi-mahi, rabbitfish, seabream, red snapper, bigeye tuna, turtle, unknown fish (10)

sushi paradise — 97
carp, wagyu cow, cuttlefish, bluefin tuna, minke whale (5)

local markets — 103
brill, aylesbury duck, monkfish, red mullet, sild, dover sole, sprat, rainbow trout, whitebait (9)

memories of the med — 109
dormouse, grouper, octopus, sardine, seabass, squid (6)

niger nibbles — 117
crocodile, rock python (2)

paddy bounty 121
rice-field rat (1)

in praise of pig 125
boar, pig, warthog (3)

lucky restaurants 131
butterfish, dog, goose, salmon, sewin, snipe, swan, brown trout, yellowfin tuna (9)

retribution 139
alligator, bear, bison, roe deer, hippopotamus, lamprey, mackerel, marlin, scorpion, shark, swordfish, tarantula (12)

safari biltong 149
impala, kangaroo, kudu, nyala, ostrich, ox, springbok, waterbuck (8)

sahara sickness 153
camel, fox, viper (3)

full list with place(s) of best meal (150) 159

introduction

Animals are multi-celled, membrane-bound organisms in the biological kingdom 'Animalia'. With few exceptions, animals eat organic material, breathe oxygen, have muscles, are able to move, can reproduce sexually and grow from a hollow sphere of cells. Animals form a *clade*, meaning that they have a single common ancestor. Over 1.5 million living animal species have been described of which around 1.05 million are insects, over 85,000 are molluscs and around 65,000 are vertebrates. It has been estimated there are as many as 7.77 million animal species on Earth. Animal body lengths range from 0.00033 inches to 110 feet. Animals have complex relationships with each other and their environments, forming intricate food chains. The scientific study of animals is known as zoology, and the study of animal behaviour is known as ethology.

Wikipedia, extract, amended 2025

This book is about a personal animal food chain: one hundred and fifty of them (and counting).

Recently, I published a book, *Glimpses of the Famous*. It followed long periods in hospital after several serious problems. I thought that my days as an author had ended.

As I lay, desperate for sleep, mind fuddled, often depressed, I played games of counting. How many countries had I visited? How many types of animals eaten? How many famous people had I met?

The last question led to the 'Glimpses' book. It contains short stories about seventy people picked from well over one hundred who qualify as 'Famous' only because they appear in *Wikipedia*. For each, I added a little extra research, background, a picture and context. Very personal, off-beat, whacky even. It would be no great novel. Just for me, really, to let me know that I would get better.

'Glimpses' was a 'dipping' book where a reader could follow their choice of a famous person and find a few pages to enjoy. While the stories would be autobiographical, the book would not be a story of my life. In fact, some of my 'famous' encounters were trivial and signified nothing other than I had met someone with a past others deemed important. All the same, each meeting held some broader interest as it dredged my memory.

To my happy surprise, the book proved popular and I was encouraged to try something similar from other musings in my hospital bed. Hence, here are another set of short stories, in the same style, from a list I built of one hundred and fifty animals that I remembered eating. Vegetarians should now turn away: I reached almost two hundred species.

Two hundred begs the obvious question, 'How many is a lot?'

I conducted a deeply-scientific, mini survey among local chefs. The answer was a surprise. For about half of restaurant goers, five is a lot. They don't eat fish, except the most sanitised fish and chips, and they abhor bones. They only order chicken, lamb, prawns and the most disguised of pork dishes: sausages, bacon, ham slices, pizza, cold pies and the like. Beef is slipping down the register.

'I bet,' said one gnarled cooker, 'that most people will never eat more than ten and they'll only get there by accident and because they have turkey at Christmas.'

The events covered go back over sixty years, if it is imaginable, to a time when there was no internet or mobile phones. Each chapter is a collection of meals, often with the briefest recipes, that concentrates as much on the context as on the courses.

I have also reflected in much more depth than intended about the reasons for eating, and for not eating, fellow animals. Writing does force re-examination. I have made myself compare the logic, ethics even, of eating, for instance, goose but not swan, cow but not horse, tuna but not whale, pig but not a human.

These stories may solve or reinforce individual positions on eating flesh, but it has not done so for me. I have shown my dilemma with a personal gesture.

An 'Elephant' stands for all the conflated arguments: it is noble, symbolic, loved, proud, cute, intelligent, caring, free and has more status than a langoustine. Yet I have seen piles of elephant meat dumped in the corner of a fly-laden abattoir, each animal having spent its life painfully hauling logs on chains many miles through forest tracks.

At the beginning of each chapter there is a list of the animals discussed within. The list never includes, for instance, the 'Elephant' but the 'elephant'. There is a choice to be made each time with each species. Are they valued fellow inhabitants or just commercial 'lower case' food?

I have remembered and researched as best I can and sometimes left things vague where there is serious doubt. There must inevitably be errors in date, place or sequence.

Not every devoured species carries an identifying image. I hope everyone knows what a sheep looks like. The pictures supporting each chapter come almost entirely from *Wikimedia Commons*, a repository of free-to-use photographs. I have given more specific credit when requested. I have also made a small contribution to *Wikipedia* in thanks.

Chris Heal
Four Marks, Hampshire
chrisheal@candspublishing.org.uk
September 2025

out of africa

anchovy, catfish, frog, horse, monkey, nile perch, nile tilapia, sandre, snail

One of the few advantages of working for a large business is that when you are travelling and staying away from home your meals are on expenses.

In the early 1980s, I worked in Johannesburg and every few months needed to fly to my company's European headquarters in Paris or to the UK or the USA. The standard flight was ten or more cramped hours overnight, slowly going mad with the tedium, the plastic food and the lack of space and sleep. There was always the unattractive prospect of flying under apartheid rules on South African Airways. These flights necessitated a midnight refuelling stop on *Ilha do Sal*, 'island of salt', in the independent Cape Verde in the central Atlantic.

The scene at *Ilha do Sal* was from a Graham Greene novel: a huge jet, the only plane on the ground; a bare, single concrete runway stretching to the horizon; the ramshackle one-horse terminal building. It was always jungle steamy and too black to see the edge of anything. The smell was aviation fuel mixed with rotting leaves. Experienced travellers wore T-shirts to soak up the sweat and had a replacement waiting on the aircraft for a quick change before attempting sleep. Bar and cleaning staff slept regardless on plastic benches meant for passengers. Occasionally the beer was cold but, more often, it was flat and warm. Geckoes played on the walls. For fifty minutes, the main sound was the crackling of cicadas and the churring of nightjars. Sometimes an unseen man shouted, short, guttural, without reply. Perhaps a metal tool echoed as it hit the floor. A seeming million pinpricks lit the heavens interrupted by steady satellites and clutches of whispering shooting stars.

I discovered the French airline UTA, *Union de Transports Aériens,* which operated intercontinentally and independent of government (with excellent food). It was part-owned by the noble Fabre family through their extensive French shipping line, *Compagnie Maritime des Chargeurs Réunis*. UTA became too profitable and therefore attractive to non-French interests. It was eventually swallowed by state-owned Air France for its own protection.

UTA seemed to go everywhere north and at unusual times of the day. One of these oddities was a weekly flight from Johannesburg to Nice which left early on a Sunday morning. How civilised and with the substantial bonus of dinner in Nice, a good hotel, a connection to Paris and all for less than the price of the conventional direct trip. For me, there was the bonus from time to time of visits to the *Musées Matisse* and *Marc Chagall*.

In Nice, I ate out just behind the *Promenades des Anglais* in the street restaurants along the *rue de France* and into the old town hinterland. If the waiters were friendly and the chat was good, I was often able to get into the kitchen to watch how a particular dish was prepared.

Salade Niçoise was my regular favourite as a counterpoint to the meat-laden South African diet. The great debate was whether to use tuna or anchovies, sadly both usually tinned. There were emotional scenes when I described the salad as a palette for experimentation rather than a dish bound by tradition. The basis was agreed: seeded fresh tomatoes, pitted black olives, gem lettuce and hard boiled eggs. I wanted halved small new potatoes, finely chopped red onion and tuna chunks and anchovy filets together, both fresh, plus crushed basil leaves before applying the *vinaigrette*.

My company's main building in Paris was in *La Défense*, in those days some fifty years ago more of a building site than the bustling hub of today as international businesses struggled patriotically to come to terms with its concrete sprawl and design oddities. My favourite restaurant was not one of the brash newcomers, but a leftover from the previous jumble of small streets underneath the vast central square. It was always cramped and never boring.

northern anchovies.
© United States Department of Commerce.

The menu seemed a deliberate challenge to any

social conformity. Visiting New Yorkers were ushered to witness the standard frog legs so that their horror could be enjoyed by the locals. The legs were imported from Vietnam, a colonial leftover, but China and Indonesia were also big exporters into France. World trade accounted for over three billion frogs a year. The restaurant served them lightly grilled with green salad or spinach. Of course, they 'tasted like mild chicken' but with a hint of fish. Frog legs are rich in all the good things like protein, omega-3 fatty acids and potassium.

The fun part for the unwary is that frog muscles handle *rigor mortis* less well than warm-blooded animals. Fresh frog legs twitch in cooking, the kitchen being open to the dining area. There were many cartoons on the walls, one showing legless frogs moving around a care home in wheelchairs.

Which brings me to horse, one of the two principal offers of the establishment. The other was *osso buco*, normally veal shanks but occasionally horse, served stewed with vegetables and white wine. The delicacy of this dish is the marrow, the *buco*, in the sliced bones, the *osso*. There was always much sucking, slurping and cleaning of hands. Outstanding.

And so to the vexed question of eating horse. I checked recently with my grandchildren which of the animals listed in this book were today universally beyond the pale. The answer was penguin, dog and horse with a few votes for rabbit, hamster and spider.

These opinions are often arbitrary and emotional and sometimes complex.

Some animals are 'just too gross' for Europeans. This group is easily typified by the fried tarantula, but might also include the human.

Other animals are 'just too cute' like penguin. In places where almost all people have enough to eat, some potential foods have crossed over from breakfast to pet. You don't eat your friends. Here live comfortably hamsters, rabbits, cats, dogs and horses. This category might be further extended to include, say, pigs, especially if you have ever witnessed farmers' heartbreak at sending their intelligent stock to the abattoir. How do you care for an animal intimately over many years, then kill it for money?

Finally, there are animals that get caught up in religion or politics or some other social force. Why were cows and chickens domesticated for consumption while cats and dogs were not? Could the survivors have had other purposes: cats to kill rodents, dogs to guard sheep and to collect game, or horses to ride or pull equipment? Why are pigs unclean and cows holy? Were some animals

flathead catfish. © Eric Engbretson.

easier to catch, more easily adapted to produce more meat, or did they just taste better?

The unlucky horse has been eaten throughout human history and across the world. The origins of the horse-eating taboo date to the year 732. Pope Gregory III issued a decree in response to Scandinavian pagan rituals of horse slaughter and sacrifice. The Pope called eating horse meat 'filthy and abominable'. Horse meat became scarce in Europe while it was integral to diets in Central Asia. It is still eaten today, for instance, as the *kazy* sausage, traditional food of Bashkirs, Kazakhs, Tatars, Kyrgyz and Uzbeks. The French Republic took a view and prioritised horses for work and declared the European landscape better suited for cows and pigs.

Prior to the 1850s in France, horse meat was considered a low-quality meat. However, in 1866, a campaign sought successfully to promote and legalize horse meat consumption. Social historians add that horses were the prized pets of the hated remaining aristocracy and may have suffered as part of a continuing revolutionary fervour. With the Prussian siege of Paris in 1870, just a few years later, citizens ate horse as well as rat and donkey when pigs and cows were expensive and in short supply.

Horse meat can still be found in France, although its popularity has been waning. Special butchers called *chevaline* sell the meat. Their numbers are dwindling. Between 2005 and 2018, the number of horse butchers fell from more than one thousand to around three hundred. The number of horses slaughtered for meat fell over ten years from eighteen thousand to under four thousand by 2022. That year, less than seven per cent of French households said they had eaten horse in the previous twelve months.

Due to its scarcity, horse is now the most expensive meat on the market. In 2021, it cost nearly €20 per kilogram compared with lamb at €17.26, veal at €17.09 and beef at €16.93.

In 2013, a horsemeat scandal sent shockwaves around the world. The Irish Food Safety Authority found horse in cheap frozen beef. Tests found that in products made for large distributors by a French company, *Comigel*, some of the so-called beef was one hundred per cent horse.

Horse meat is very lean and care must be taken not to over dry it during cooking. The meat is tasty and sweet and contains twice as much iron as beef for the pot. Horse presentation, therefore, goes in two directions, both of which were regularly available and easily prepared in my *La Défense* restaurant: the first was raw or nearly raw like thinly-sliced *carpaccio*, steak tartare or rare steak, or, second, as well-sauced red wine stews.

During one visit to Nice, there was a crisis at the airport, a gunman, I think, and I made a dash for the station and caught a train to Lyon. Here I walked the narrow *traboules* of the old town. Hundreds of these passages crisscross the city's courtyards, built by the silk merchants to keep their goods dry. Of course, they also lead to interesting restaurants.

My choice that evening was snails, crawling with butter and garlic, followed by *sandre*, or pikeperch (it's a perch), the freshwater fish of the Loire. As with most fish, there's a need to make sure that it is from the wild, *sauvage*. Don't be fooled by the chemical-filled soups that house loch salmon in Scotland and German-run seabream and seabass farms in Greece. Wild *sandre* are usually quite big (around six kilograms compared to about two from a farm) so the fish is often served in fillets. It is white, delicate and firm with few bones and well worth a try. This one came with asparagus, button mushrooms and a Bechamel sauce.[1]

I mentioned that UTA offered some unexpected flights from Johannesburg. One of these was to Paris via Cairo and, by carefully shuffling my calendar, I was able to tie my trip into a short River Nile cruise.

While waiting for my connection to the river boat, I arranged for a taxi to take me to the Egyptian Museum to see, among much else, Pharaoh Tutankhamun's treasure, including his iconic gold burial mask. It was odd that when the driver took me to the main door the guard bowed and touched his feet in a sign of respect. When the man stood before the museum's copy of the Rosetta Stone and freely translated its texts in hieroglyphic and Demotic Ancient Egyptian and, at the bottom, in Ancient Greek, I could hold back no longer.

nile perch. © Smudger888.

---

1 Infused milk (onion, bay leaf, cloves, nutmeg), butter and flour.

The cabbie was a touch bashful.

'This is the first day of my new job,' he explained. 'You are my first customer. Yesterday, I was the museum director, but I have retired.'

The Nile boat presented as a studiously renovated Victorian slice of time, but I felt on inspection that, though the shiny brass work and highly polished wood were impressive, the Victorian structure actually hid a more shabby, modern piece of work. Don't get me wrong. The service was good to second class and the archaeological sites were breathtaking even if the accompanying talks were book learned and robotic. You get what you pay for.

I always get grumpy when I'm trapped and the food is disappointing, in this case unimaginative. Each night was the same, an extensive buffet which was little more than piles of standard Europeanised offerings that could be bought anywhere. I decided to get off the boat and try something local. We berthed at a small town in Upper Egypt, the name now escapes me. As is usual with these 'exclusive' tours, the boat was fourth from shore.

The crew fought me all the way. When I left the boat, I would slip between the other craft on the way to the jetty and die horribly. I would get lost in the night. While I was lost I would get mugged. There was no good hospital within a hundred kilometres. I would certainly get food poisoning. There would be no alcohol. Mosquitoes and unknown insects would give me a fatal disease. Any local restaurant would up their prices. The boat would leave without me and I would miss all my connections. The purser was called. The captain was called. The two couples who had decided to join me cried off, each announcement greeted with tears of joy and sighs of relief.

It was a pleasant enough town with attempts at flower beds in the centre of the dusty main road. There was little traffic and some of the streetlights worked. Passers by waved or called *As-salamu alaikum*, 'peace be upon you' or *Marhaban*, 'welcome'. Twice, I was asked into homes for mint tea and friendly interrogation which neighbours rushed to join while children stared through chinks in the curtained doorway.

I was taken to a restaurant on the open roof of a small hotel where I was introduced to the owner. He looked villainous with squint eyes, occasional teeth and a black fez and matching wide belt. He grasped both my hands in his and welcomed me warmly. Two men from my home visits stayed in the background for ten minutes to make sure things went well. The view across the river was stunning, the menu was a delightful English approximation and the sky, as ever, blue-dark and star-spangled. I had a ringside seat. Most other tables were taken but only mine received a special white linen cloth laid with elaborate ceremony. Water was brought for hand washing. Two old men played their lutes quietly behind a drape.

nile tilapia.
© Germano Roberto Schüür.

I ate olives with local oil, a type of humous, cracked walnuts and warm unleavened bread. Cold beer appeared. I was assured that further bottles were nearby as the capacity of the English was well known. There were frequent muted calls of 'Manchester United' and 'Bobby Charlton' followed by a chuckle and a thumbs up.

The manager advised a combination of two fish caught that day in front of the hotel. He sought out the English names in a tired book: *bulṭi*, 'Nile tilapia' which was dark-fleshed and fried whole, and a large steak of *capitaine*, 'Nile perch', a cannibalistic fish which grows up to two metres, almost boneless, white and surprisingly sweet. They were served side-by-side with potatoes and spiced kale. Tilapia was on my bucket list. The day before I had seen one on a tomb wall painting of man-made fish ponds from several thousand years ago.

It was an excellent excursion. Back on the boat, one crew member insisted on squeezing my arms to ensure that I had returned alive and well.

One UTA flight, this time direct to Paris, made an unscheduled stop with a suspected engine fault at Maya-Maya airport in the centre of Brazzaville. The city, the capital of the Republic of the Congo, lies on the Congo River. On the facing bank is the city of Kinshasa, the capital of the Democratic Republic of the Congo, frequently a warring opponent.

It was not a good time to drop in unannounced. The runway was lined with sleek jet fighters, ready for action. Troops, many of them boy soldiers, slouched everywhere, all armed to the teeth and beyond. It was teeming with rain which never stopped. I was happy to be transferred after an hour or so to some western multi-storey hotel. I had to share a room with a morose man with a large drooping moustache who placed his pistol on the table by his bed. He insisted I ate with him at a place he knew. The food was 'monkey' done it a curry stew. I never knew what sort of monkey. It was gamey, but palatable. I didn't argue or comment, but drank *Ngok*, 'crocodile' lager from green bottles, switched to whisky and caught a taxi back. I never saw my roommate again. By midday, the plane was fixed, a faulty alarm, and I made my meeting in Paris a day late.

UTA also flew me once to Florida with a brief refuelling stop in the Azores. I think it was a trial flight and I never saw it advertised again. I was visiting a manufacturing plant in Boca Raton to discuss marketing a new product. At Miami International Airport on a Saturday mid-afternoon, my hosts asked if I would like to go fishing.

It was a little over an hour's drive to the Everglades in American luxury, a very large camping truck with all the gear. My three friends settled us into a rented wood cabin and we sat in rocking chairs on the netted porch and drank beer and rye whiskey and ate fresh fried prawn po' boy sandwiches till late. Outside our sanctuary, all manner of wildlife screamed madly like demented ghosts for most of the night.[2]

I can't honestly remember much of the following day. We had a flatbottomed boat with a small cabin and two enormous outboards. And, of course, two televisions and a serious bar. Drinking started with the engines. We were in St Johns River, several hundred kilometres long before it met the Atlantic in Jacksonville, I think in the section between Palatka and Lake George. The fish leapt aboard in droves: channel catfish, bullhead and a few white catfish. We spent a lot of time near deep holes at river bends. One of my channel catfish was almost a metre long caught with crab bait. I couldn't keep up with the slang names: mud cat, polliwogs and chuckleheads. I had to learn to dodge the spines which could inflict severe wounds. Gloves were usually worn for handling.

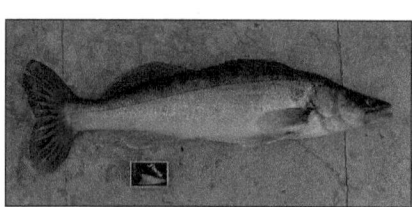

sandre. © eLNuko

My fellow fishermen were serious and were stocking for the freezer and the market.

That night, we ate channel catfish crumbed with cornmeal and fried. My hosts pronounced the catch 'excellent'. The meat is evidently widely popular. I found my steak a little watery and lacking in flavour, but I kept quiet. I was

---

2 A po' boy (poor boy), derived from southern accents, is a sandwich originally from Louisiana. It traditionally consists of a filling, which is usually roast beef, ham, or fried seafood such as shrimp, crawfish, fish, oysters, or crab, on a New Orleans French bread roll, cut lengthwise. Po' boy bread is known for its crisp crust and fluffy crumb (*Wikipedia* 2025).

disappointed, but not too bothered. It was a top, unexpected day out. There was still plenty of po' boy around.

A few years later, President Ronald Reagan proclaimed a National Catfish Day because the fish was such a staple.

crawly things

weaver ant larva, stink bug, house cricket, short-tailed cricket, grasshopper, wasp larva, palm weevil.

Lao people have always eaten insects which are generally regarded as *saep laai laai*, 'delicious'. The animals are collected in the fields and forests around homes. Any excess is sold to local restaurants and markets. If you do eat out, the usual rule applies especially in areas when there is limited or no electricity for refrigeration. Trust your nose. Most insects are deep fried and only one, the herbivorous stink bug, *mieng keng*, is eaten raw with sticky rice. These bugs secrete a foul-smelling substance from pores in their sides which colours collectors' hands yellow. If you see a Laotian scrambling in a tree trunk with plastic gloves on, you'll know what's up.

Farming insects is a relatively new practice which began under a United Nations programme with two cricket species, the short-tailed or field cricket, *chi nai*, and the domestic house cricket, *chi lor*. The short-tail needs to be dug out of its burrow using a small spade. It is most common in the last three months of the year. A few days before harvesting, the domestic version is fed with pumpkin or other vegetables and the females are offered plastic bowls with a mixture of sand and burned rice husks in which to lay their eggs. *Chi lor* just gets the popular taste vote as well as having the better chance of being fresh.[3]

adult red palm weevil. © Kemel49.

---

3   Hanboonsong, Yupa, and Durst, Patrick B, 'Edible Insects in Lao PDR' (Food and Agriculture Organization of the United Nations 2014).

I arrived at the *River Resort* hotel on the banks of the wide Mekong in southern Laos, near to the small town of *Champasak*. Not too far away is one of the oldest temples in Southeast Asia, *Wat Phou*, a spectacular site that sits amidst rice fields. It boasts a very old canal which was built by the rulers of the Khmer empire before the construction of the world-famous *Angkor Wat*. The temple is in three levels: the first focusses on the *baray*, a water reservoir and promenade, the second features quadrangular pavilions and galleries of carvings and the top is the sanctuary itself.

It was very hot. I cooled in the sacred spring, once part of a Hindu temple. After a short, steep climb, I paused by the Crocodile Stone where volunteer virgins were sacrificed to appease *Shiva*.

A local driver with good French and a smattering of American attached himself. He was short, dressed in worn jeans and a *Coca-Cola* T-shirt, and sported a thatch of black hair and red facial scars. A respectful distance away stood an even smaller young woman with coiled shiny hair.

'*Big fight. Strong tiger. Me called* Mee, *mean 'bear',* he offered with a smile pointing to his scars. '*She my wife. She called* Goong. *Mean 'shrimp'. Tastes good. True, yes? Helps lots with food and travel. We big love.*'

Wherever I went, there they were, not pushy, but helpful and determined.

As I dropped down to the promenade again, beginning to fill with coaches of tourists, *Mee* answered my prayers.

'*You look hot. Walk long way. I show you good café. You need cold beer. Mebbe two.*'

I thanked him. He accepted an orange drink for himself and *Goong*.

'I want to go *Sipandon*, land of four thousand islands,' I said.

'*Tomorrow*,' he said. '*Need two cars and two boats to reach this place. You chosen wise. Beautiful area of Mekong. Fourteen kilometres one side to other. Thousands of small islands. Plenty nice places to stay.*'

'I have only one day free,' I said. 'But I want something else as well. I want to eat insects like crickets and weaver ants and weevils. Do you know of such a place?'

He smiled as if at a private joke.

'*Grasshoppers, too*,' he said, giving a little demonstrative leap. '*Get you at hotel at eight? Breakfast on road. Goong make. Plenty shrimp with Goong. Speciality. Leave early for big day in islands.*'

We agreed the equivalent of £50 and that I would leave him with a full tank of petrol.

We drove back to *Champasak* where *Mee* stopped abruptly in the middle of the empty, dusty street.

'*Like good massage?*' he asked. '*Nice lady. French. She look after local girls like my sister. I wait. Take hour.*'

Was this where the relationship was to break down in some sleazy mosquito pit in a dim, dirty room? I needn't have worried. The big sign behind the welcome table read, 'Please don't ask for sex.' As always, these signs can have at least two meanings. There were lotus blossoms and cool spaces everywhere. Everything was spotless.

'*Mee* sent me,' I said.

'*Mee!* C'est un bon garçon. S'il vous plaît, venez par ici, enlevez vos vêtements et portez ce pantalon spécial.'

Next morning, we drove a short distance. River mists slowly cleared as we paddled in a small dragon boat across the Mekong to the village of *Ban Muang* to be met by a comfortable minibus driven by *Goong*, all but empty of petrol. I realised that a minibus took a lot of fuel. It took ninety minutes to reach *Ban Hatsaikhone*, but not before I had eaten delicious *Zhong Zhong Ngo Hiang*, shrimp fritter cakes, and we had run over a dog.

'*Sorry bout dog*,' said Mee. '*Plenty dogs die on this crazy road. Lazy. Lie in middle in hot sun. Villagers no help. Dog die, people eat them. We stop they get angry. Ask for stupid money. Big scam.*'

We took a local boat for another ninety minutes to the serene islands of *Don Det* and *Don Khon*. I caught a glimpse of the fins of two rare Irrawaddy dolphins. At the island of *Det*, an American woman slipped when stepping ashore and broke her leg. We left her with villagers lying on the roadside in obvious discomfort waiting for the local doctor.

At *Don Khon*, a tropical dream of rice paddies with hues of jade and emerald, we walked in the shade of teaks along the river bank: water buffalo, long-tailed macaques and red-necked keelbacks sunned by

red weaver ant. © Muhammad Mahdi Karim.

short-tailed crickets.

the water edge. I saw two cars, a few tuk-tuks and, for once, was free of the whine of the ubiquitous motorbike. The sleepy simple town contained a handful of French colonial houses and many smaller lodging places. The sweet smell of weed clung in the air. Contented young Europeans were everywhere, resting, chatting and smoking. I realised I was in a hippie paradise.

'Visit railway before lunch?' suggested *Mee*. *Goong* had slipped away.

The railway, including a concrete viaduct, remained largely intact although its rails had been removed. French colonialists were determined to use the Mekong River for a route from Laos, through Cambodia and into China to help counter British expansion in Upper Burma. The main obstacle was at *Sipandon* where the river divides into several channels with serious rapids. Three attempts in the 1890s to scale the falls failed. Steamships with 'engines roaring and boilers near bursting, with hundreds of men hauling from the rocks on ropes and others pushing from the decks with pikes' slid back down the slopes.

An alternative was needed. The French settled on a small portage train across the island of Don Khon and, later, Don Det, that would allow specially-designed vessels to be dismantled, transported on the railway, reassembled and launched further upstream.

The first four kilometres were laid in 1893. The railway was temporary for its first four years, laid in segments which could be lifted when the train had passed and re-laid in front. The gun sloops *Lagrandière*, *Ham Luong* and *Massie* were the first to cross the island. A permanent railway was laid by 1897 with trains with a maximum of twelve cars consisting of a steam locomotive, open-topped wagons and carriages. The outbreak of World War Two sealed the railway's fate; the last train reportedly ran in 1940.

Marthe Bassenne, a physician's wife, travelled in 1910:

> *The train, struggling and grating amid the clashing sound of steel, hauled us across the island, which is covered by teak trees and bamboos whose*

branches brushed our faces. The temperature was very high and the sun, filtering through the trees, roused noxious fever-vapours from the tangled undergrowth. Sweat caked my hair under my sun hat; the heat burned my arms through my clothes; and the mosquitoes took advantage of my predicament to attack me as they pleased, all over my hands and face...[4]

At Ban Khon village on Don Khon, I found the only steam locomotive still in existence in Laos at a former maintenance depot. Built in 1911 and named *Eloïse*, the rusty engine sits on a short stretch of track. A shed tries to protect the locomotive from further deterioration.

'Now, we eat,' said *Mee*. That secret smile came back.

We walked to the river at the edge of town. Here was a clean structure of clay blocks and bamboo open on three sides to the elements with bright plastic tables and chairs, palm leaves shading the sun. In the centre, beaming, was *Goong*.

'*My restaurant,*' explained *Mee*, hugely enjoying my surprise. '*Goong make work. Try new things. Sell only insects. What sort you want? Start with beer?*'

I settled on the insect equivalent of a mixed grill or *thali* with lots of small portions.

Both sorts of cricket came pan fried with herbs (lovely). I reckoned lemongrass, bergamot leaves, galangal, shredded pandanus leaves and cloves and then some chicken stock. Next up was an omelette of weaver ants and their eggs, cooked like at home only with lemongrass, chillies and fish sauce (I thought the chilli outdid any ant taste). The pan-roasted grasshoppers were served simply with lemon and crushed garlic (yummy and crunchy although the little legs do get stuck in your teeth). Steamed wasp larvae (perhaps the tastiest) were served in their nest which you leave. Fried palm weevils were offered with plentiful basil leaves and coconut milk, cloves and chillies (perhaps second best).

The final dish was the raw stink bug on rice. I give this a serious taste warning. Stink bug could give culinary insects a bad name.

Mee had one last surprise before we set out for home, earning his money twice over.

---

4   Keay, John, *Mad About The Mekong: Exploration and Empire in South-East Asia* (Harper 2006), pp. 80-85.

cooked stink bugs.

A local nutritionist and friend, a wiry doctor in his sixties, turned up seeking a European convert. For the price of a beer, he lamented that I had not had time or capacity to try dragonfly lava, scarab beetles, dung weevils or, even, bamboo worms (supposedly double yummy). My insect education was only half complete.

'Just take the message home,' he said in his impeccable New York accent. 'Your people have forgotten our war, but much land still can't be cultivated because of unexploded American bombs. Most of the harvesting is done while tending crops in the fields that are left. Just under half of our children under five are severely undernourished with protein and energy deficiencies. These insects give us protein, of course, but also fatty acids, vitamins and minerals.

'These kids, these insects, they are the future.'

diving delights

barnacle, crawfish, conger eel, horse mussel, lobster, razor fish, scallop, queenie scallop, sea urchin

For several years, I lived on the west coast of Scotland and dived the seas around the Clyde islands and up the lochs to the Inner Hebrides. It was a free for all in those days: rudimentary but efficient and affordable equipment, open access to the water with limited regulation and oversight. Now, if you check the host of well-meaning rules, it's a wonder any of us survived. Supervision and warning is everywhere. Calculated risk, as with travel and politics, has all but been driven out from thought and practice.

Don't do this without coming on our course! It might be dangerous! If you are stupid, you might die! Take our qualification! Don't harm the environment! Buy this! Buy that! Pass legislation! Start compulsory registration! Demand record keeping! Introduce wardens! Inform on people you've never met! Ban and fine! Socially exclude! Make the world a safer place!

A Swedish expert in some arcane software was urgently needed at my company's factory. I took a phone call from my managing director. As a reward for him catching the next plane to Scotland could someone take him diving during his short visit, meaning the following afternoon?

It was a beautiful day, the weather fine, sea like a snooker table, no wind. I chugged the borrowed inflatable with my guest and a couple of friends out into the estuary. There was a patch of rocky coast on the west of the island of Little Cumbrae, a new spot, but long on my 'most promising' list; no TV aerial or traffic jam in sight. We threw the anchor a safe distance from some jagged kelp-covered edges, popped a bottle of gin on a rope into the sea to cool, and flipped backwards into five metres of clear water.

Multi-coloured wrasse lazed among seaweed stems. A spiny dogfish pushed past, focussed on prey, but oblivious to us. Childlike bubbles floated without care

giant conger eel.

to the surface. We fell into a swarm of queen scallops. 'Queenie's' are small versions of the traditional scallop with multi-coloured shells, well worth the eating if only in tiny bites. When chased they shoot upwards, flapping madly and squirting water backwards for propulsion each time the shell snaps shut. After a few minutes, they sink again, exhausted, to land calmly into the sand, flat shell upwards. Only the slight half-moon disturbance on the speckled bottom hints at their presence. A few dozen or more were netted for later.

We were quickly among the rocks, a metre high, covered in waving fronds, red and yellow lichens and full of crevices and hideaways.

Lobsters are inquisitive animals. They back into sandy-bottom holes and wait for prey with the telltale tips of their blue claws just visible in the darkness. A diving knife tapped steadily onto their roof will prove irresistible. Patience. Settle to the bottom, lie still, breathing controlled. First, the blue claws. Keep tapping. Then the head. Poise a hand above and behind. Then the body. Grab the lobster by the shoulders and drop it tail first into your waiting net bag. My guest took one while I took the other. His excitement was palpable.

On shore, we lit a small wood fire, opened the gin, added tonic and lemon, placed the first lobster into a warming bucket of seawater and set about opening and cleaning the queenies. These were placed carefully in an open shell with butter and a thin slice of garlic to fry for a few seconds around the fire edge. Add a few crisp bread rolls, find a comfortable boulder and listen to the silence. Magic day.

There is no fish, no shell fish, like fresh fish. Foreswear the expensive, chewy, reheated lobster served in restaurants which is all sauce and no substance. Eat crab: tastier and cheaper. Lobster just out of the sea is so subtle, so delicious, that if you have ever been at a place like Little Cumbrae you would only ever buy direct from a fisherman on the quayside.

Time for home. The moon was up, the lobsters gone, every scallop slurped, sucked and slithered.

The outboard wouldn't start.

Much swearing and wasted lanyard pulling. Eventually our Swedish chum showed his engineering background. The spark plugs were unscrewed, wrapped in silver paper and placed in the coolest part of the embers to warm. Finally, one fired and on a single cylinder we crawled the couple of kilometres to the mainland.

A murmuring crowd waited on us: the distraught inflatable owner, various wives and girlfriends, managers from the factory worried about their software and the lifeboat crew about to put to sea.

'All's well. Is the pub still open?'

A few weeks later, I received my 'thank you'. A small parcel containing a piece of oak arrived from Sweden. This wood was part of a timber from the warship *Wasa* sunk at the beginning of her maiden voyage in 1628 in Stockholm Harbour. Because of the cold water and lack of Toledo worms, the oak is as resistant to a fingernail dent today as it was four hundred years ago.

A word of warning. Lobsters often share their holes with conger eel. These beasts can grow into two metre monsters. The first you know is that a black jaw full of teeth is coming out of the murk. The jaws dislocate, widen, and could take the side of a human head. You have to freeze otherwise you invite attack. For many years my *Neoprene* diving helmet boasted a deep scar over one ear where the conger's sandpaper skin had gouged a long furrow. The eel took a long time to pass.

I shot a conger once and took it back to shore, the spear straight through its little brain. It lay there inert on the quayside until someone poked it. The eel took off the tip of the finger. As retribution, I cut off the head. The perennial problem was skinning the conger. Outside my home was a lamppost to which I tied some of its black skin. I fixed the conger's body to the rear bumper of my car and drove off slowly. The fish peeled but not before the lamppost was forever bent at a funny angle and the bumper took on a new shape.

Conger is best eaten as chowder. Chunk as much flesh as you need, debone it as best you can, leaving in the backbone. Make a soup with water, white wine, cloves, bay leaves, onion, carrot, celery and all the herbs you fancy. Then add the conger chunks and cook for up to a half hour or until the fish starts to break down. Place in individual serving dishes and, at the last minute, add cooked new potatoes, cream and whisked egg yolk.

It's actually quite good!

That year, the diving group decided on a holiday in Angle in west Wales. First dive, I spotted a crawfish, a new species for me, a very good-looking animal, orange golden colour and covered in spines. The surprise was that, although a relative to the lobster and roughly the same size, it had no claws. It was crawling along a sandy bottom in plain sight. The internet today claims crawfish was close to eradication in UK waters due to widespread capture by divers and netters in the 1960s and 70s. If so, I am guilty as charged with my one catch, but it could have tried a bit harder to escape. I also found, without exception, that commercial shellfish fishermen always blamed divers for shortages, including theft from pots. I never witnessed any thieving and never saw that many divers in those early days.

My crawfish had a splendid, more subtle taste than lobster after being cooked the same way.

The next day in almost the same spot, I found the largest sea urchins I have ever seen. I was used to them in Scotland, but these monsters were up to three times the size. Urchins have some unexpected relatives. The closest is the sea cucumber which I found off the Normandy coast. The next is the almost flat sand dollar whose shells I discovered in large quantities in the Kalahari Desert.

After the dive, I sat, back against a sea wall and used my knife to scrape off the urchins' spines. These spines are the greatest threat to humans who unsuspectedly tread on them. The results can be painful and serious as some are poisonous and can cause breathing problems, especially in the West Indies. I then scooped out the mouth-come-feet which live together in the apical disc, a hole underneath the shell. Inside were strips of orange roe which I collected. Unexpectedly, I found I had a business. Tourists offered me £5 for each shell. Four of them paid for dinner. Another made a lamp shade.

These lengths of roe are nothing of the sort; they are gonads, the urchin's sex organs. They are eaten raw in *sushi* and *sashimi* with soy sauce and *wasabi* which is how I tried half of them: salty, full of flavour, not unlike the sudden burst of a caviar egg. The other half I fried quickly and lightly in butter with a small amount of chopped shallot and garlic and ate on thin toast. Both methods definitely moved onto my menu.

I was sobered when I found that, at today's prices, the Japanese pay £500 a kilogram for top quality sea urchin gonads.

The sea got its own back that night. The group was staying in caravans. The nearby pub had odd opening hours because it could only be reached across a tidal causeway. I was on babysitting duty for the first hour or so and lent my Cortina estate to a friend. At first I thought the knock at the door was a joke, but then realised that his wife was serious. My friend, now in hiding, anxious not to miss his beer had turned too soon off the causeway which he tried to drive across as the tide washed in. You could see my yellow car quite clearly lying on the bottom with its lights on. I suggested to him he might like to join it.

It was a welcome challenge for the pub's clientele. When the tide dropped, twelve good men and true lifted the car by hand back onto the road. It started first time.

And then, the car saga went full circle. The same group was staying near Achiltibuie by the mouth of Loch Broom on the Scottish west coast. Our plan was to dive the Summer Isles, a wild and multi-islanded place and, from what we could gather, little dived.

The waters were as clear as any around the UK, but strangely shy of fish. On the second dive, we found an extensive bed of king scallops. These shellfish, *pecten maximus*, are larger versions of queenies. Their shells are often sold to tourists in the seaside resorts. The white flesh is sweet and succulent and an expensive option on good menus in season before everything became frozen and foreign. The large orange and red roe can also be fried and served whole or used to make a fine sauce.

We took enough shellfish for dinner and asked the chef at the local posh hotel if he would cook them for us. He asked whether there were many more to be found. We spent the next two days diving for his freezer. I made enough money to buy a replacement car.

The sandy beaches on the islands also provided a plentiful source of

razor fish. © Britishseafishing.

barnacles and razor fish. There's no need for SCUBA gear as they can be picked up on the shoreline.[5]

The trick with barnacles is to choose those that spend most of their lives under water that is clean and free from human sewage and engine oil. Flick them off the rocks with a thin flat knife. You can knock them off with a stone, but once alerted they suck down hard and you might as well give up. They are good raw and I usually eat a few this way, but for me are best boiled for ten minutes and served with a tomato sauce (onion, celery, garlic, white wine) and tossed in a bed of spaghetti or noodles.

Collecting razor fish, or clams, can be more fun. When you see their empty shells, perhaps six inches long like a thin pencil case, lying on the beach, you're in the right place. The animal lives under the sand and drags itself down by inflating and anchoring its foot and then deflating while squirting water into its hole to remove loose sand from its path. Look for key-hole shaped depressions in the sand made as the razor feeds on plankton. A teaspoon of salt into the hole persuades the fish that the tide has come in and up it pops.

sea urchin. © Nick Hopgood.

Razor fish are best cooked the same day, but overnight in the fridge will do little harm. Treat them like delicate clams. Place them in boiling water. In a few seconds, the shells will open. Drain right away and put them into cold water to keep them from cooking and becoming tough. Peel the long, cylindrical body from the shell and snip off the tough foot. Split lengthwise and clean.

Serve as a rice and vegetable stir-fry with onion, garlic, ginger and, perhaps, Chinese five-spice or Indian *garam masala*. Alternatively, sauté the strips quickly in butter and garlic and

---

5   Self-contained underwater breathing apparatus.

serve them with chopped parsley and lemon wedges. They can also be battered and served with chips. The flesh should be white and sweet, more lobster than clam to the taste.

One day, looking for new dive sites only accessible from an inflatable, we found some sheer cliffs near Lochgilphead, a small town at the end of the loch near the start of the Crinan Canal, a fifteen kilometre connection to the Isle of Jura. On the cliffs' tidal area was a mass of clinging horse mussels, far beyond anything I had seen before. These mussels grow up to eight inches of so. A handful make a meal. We knew them as 'clabby-doos', in Gaelic *clabaidh-dubha* or 'big black mouths'. They just need a bit longer cooking than ordinary mussels.

The sides of the loch were steep. On a ledge ten metres down, we found the wreck of an aged fishing boat, seemingly undamaged, masts and sails in place, a haunt for crustaceans.

I heard later that some unscrupulous divers had used these cliffs to drop three old cars, stripped of petrol and oil sumps, into the sea, guiding them by inflatable bags so that they sat on each other to make a reef. The cars were surrounded by tins of cat food, each opened only at one spot so that the smell rather than the meat could seep out.

Lobsters love *Kitekat*.

the great elephant cull

elephant

There are fashions in the conservation business just like in any other endeavour that needs to make money. One of the biggest and most deadly happened in the Kruger National Park, a a large and diverse place which today manages almost twenty thousand square kilometres in the north east corner of South Africa. It is three hundred and sixty kilometres long with an average width of sixty-five kilometres bordered by the Limpopo River in the north, by Moçambique in the east and by the Crocodile River in the south. There are other great rivers that run through: the Sabie, Olifants, Letaba and Levuvhu.

Many of the good tar roads that take you deep into the bush to see the game from your car have much more to do with speeding military convoys to these once highly sensitive borders during the age of apartheid than for any love of tourists.

The Park, opened in 1918, resulted from a Game Commission established in 1891, but the wish to preserve wildlife goes back to at least 1867 when some two hundred farmers issued notices protecting game on their three hundred farms.

The Kruger's highly emotive fashion concerns the perceived effect on vegetation of the Park's elephant herds and what to do about it.[6] Elephants can seem to be hugely destructive, ripping down trees and leaving empty landscapes.

Elephants, the largest living land animals, also have prodigious memories and have many reasons to hate humans. They have been trained, seemingly against their wishes, to kill in war or to execute in peace by stomping. And, yet,

---

6 Pinnock, Don, 'The myth of too many elephants in Kruger Park, and why culling is redundant', *The Journal of African Elephants*, 23/7/2022.

talk to any visitor to Thai or Sri Lankan tourist sanctuaries and you will hear very different and more pleasant stories.

Around the end of the nineteenth century in southern Africa there was ivory hunting carnage. The elephant was almost wiped out. When the practice was curtailed by legislation, animals started to drift back into the old Kruger Park. By 1938, there were an estimated four hundred elephant and the number kept growing. In the 1960s, Park management decided there were too many and recommended culling. A thumb suck suggested one elephant a square mile, a maximum of seven thousand.

Conservationist Don Pinnock offers the view that the idea of a 'right number' of elephants within a reserve is a 'moving target', depending on personal opinion formed through experiences, anecdotes, numbers, rates of growth, limited visual impressions and hearsay.

I regularly visited the Park in the 1980s and, as a result of the cull, often enjoyed elephant *biltong*, a bit like beef, but nothing untoward. I ate elephant steak in a Kruger Park lodge charcoaled on a mix of acacia, *sekelbos* and stink wood after the meat had been well marinaded. It was slightly stringier than beef.

By 1995, after almost thirty years of culling, 14,629 elephants had been killed and a large abattoir built at Skukuza to process the mountains of meat. Amid growing public disgust, the slaughter brought a global backlash and was stopped.

For the first time, serious research was conducted into elephants and their habitats. The findings showed that the elephant is the Kruger Park's 'constant gardener' widely transporting seeds and is a creator of 'browsing lawns' of low height essential for other herbivores.

By 2021, there were almost thirty thousand elephants, nowhere near close to reassessed theoretical Park limits.

The Kruger has not been trashed and there is no plan to reintroduce the cull.

fish'n'chips'n'biafra

cod, coley, spiny dogfish, gurnard, haddock, hake, halibut, kingklip, lumpfish, pollock, snoek, sturgeon, tilapia, whiting

Battered fish and chunky chips was the national dish of the United Kingdom until the arrival of curry in the 1970s. It is also the top takeaway in many other English-speaking countries. The British government safeguarded the supply of fish and chips during the two world wars by not introducing rationing. George Orwell in *The Road to Wigan Pier* in 1937 considered fish and chips chief among the 'home comforts which acted as a panacea to the North of England working classes'. There were over thirty-five thousand frying shops in the 1930s, now down to under ten thousand. Today, the UK's 'chippies' sell roughly twenty-five per cent of all white fish and ten per cent of all potatoes in the country.

Traditionally, the meal was served on old newspapers with a splash of vinegar and a dash of salt. Posh people, who sat down to eat, might add mushy peas, bread and butter, a pickled onion or egg, a slice of lemon and, most importantly, a cup of strong tea. Nowadays, any number of differently-coloured sauces, from tartar to tomato, and drinks, from cola to water, are standard, plus battered vegan sausages, chicken pieces, burgers and even, in Glasgow, *Mars* bars.

The fish is filleted and, hopefully, all the bones removed. The batter, usually a simple water or beer and flour mix, is dropped into either beef dripping or vegetable oil, with

cod. © Hans-Petter Fjeld.

heritage interests favouring lard. Oils, like palm, rape and peanut, cater for vegetarians and certain faiths. The busiest fish and chips day is Friday with more than a nod to the Roman Catholic practice of a meat-less day.

Because I grew up just after World War Two, my common fish was 'rock salmon', a cover name for the spiny dogfish, a small shark, which mongers thought if correctly named might frighten customers away. I got to love the taste. Many years later, diving in the Clyde estuary, dogfish were a common sight, up to a metre long, swimming lazily above the seabed. Their egg sacks clung to the seaweed or floated free. If you grabbed a tail, the dogfish would lunge away a few times then turn to face you and you had to hold your nerve as it wrapped around your arm and played dead. I often dived with a dogfish on each arm, showing off to newcomers. As soon as I broke the surface, they flipped and were gone.

Of course, the great fish and chip favourite is cod, the monarch of the North Atlantic, with its mild flavour and dense, flaky white flesh which holds together well in the fryer. Slightly upmarket for some, is the haddock, preferred in Scotland, clean and white and similar to cod. The Finnan haddie and the Arbroath smokie are versions smoked in oak chips.

Other regulars in the London chippies of my youth were coley, pollock and whiting, but around the world I have found many more: I've had hake and snoek in South Africa, gurnard in New Zealand, halibut and tilapia in the USA and seen countless other species on offer. European busybodies now declaim that 'fish and chips' is illegal and that, in store, fish species must be specified. The great cod substitute in southern Africa is kingklip, not a fish, but a deep water cusk eel, in my opinion, better tasting. White, thick flaked, the kingklip is also brilliant in a curry.

The names of frying establishments can be fun: 'A Salt and Battery', 'The Codfather', 'The Frying Scotsman', 'Rock and Sole' and 'Jack the Chipper'.

In 1967, the Smiths Potato Crisps Company created salt and vinegar flavoured crisps in the UK, inspired by fish and chips, and thus ruined bar snacks for ever.

I haven't yet mentioned my favourite fish and chips meal: cod roe. The roe is delivered compressed in round tins, the 'cake' then chopped into thick slices and battered in the normal way. Cod roe, and the eggs of other fish, can also be bought over the fishmonger counter in its original state and is delicious quick fried in butter and drizzled with lemon juice.

My liking for cod roe brought me to lumpfish caviar, a cheap substitute for the real thing, sold in small jars in supermarkets. Lumpfish are plump fish, mainly from the North Atlantic; their large egg sacks are a major prize. The eggs are salted and coloured red or black. They are also used as a 'cleaner fish' to reduce the parasite burden on salmon farms in Scottish lochs.

For a tasty treat, butter bite-sized circles of thin toast then layer a slice of boiled egg, a dollop of lumpfish caviar and top with a tiny sprig of parsley, the whole sprinkled in black pepper. A dozen will do the job.

And, so that I can add sturgeon to my list of eaten animals, a small cheat. I once had proper caviar for lunch in the *Savoy Grill* in London, paid for by a rich client. It was served on thin soldiers of buttered toast. Soft and fresh, it had an unexpected buttery flavour that exploded in the mouth as I bit into the sockets. The big surprise is that each egg tastes differently from its neighbour. That snack was the real deal and one day I must get a birthday delivery not intended for sharing. At the *Savoy*, I finished with a crème brûlée to die for (in fact, I ate two).

Fish and chips used to be sold in separate establishments in Victorian England. The practice may have been introduced by Iberian Jews who immigrated from the Netherlands as early as the sixteenth century to near the Spitalfields area of London. Charles Dickens mentions 'fried fish warehouses' in *Oliver Twist* in 1838 and, by 1859, talks in *A Tale of Two Cities* of 'husky chips of potato, fried with some reluctant drops of oil'. Fish and chips became an English stock meal after the rapid development of trawl fishing in the North Sea. The building of the railways from the ports to the industrial cities in the fifty years to 1900 brought the fish quickly to hungry mouths with limited money.

In 1928, Harry Ramsden opened his first fish and chip shop in Guiseley, West Yorkshire, but there has been fierce debate since as to the identity of the very first 'first.'

spiny dogfish. © Doug Costa, NOAA/SBNMS.

And, so, a return to the cod and to the serious part of this humble story.

For reasons you can find elsewhere, I was flying transport planes into the Biafran war zone in the late 1960s.[7]

On an early trip, I left Faro in Portugal at the beginning of April in an ageing ex-Luftwaffe C-47 Dakota. I found it sitting forlorn on the tarmac alongside some RAF-surplus Meteor jets. With me was a sixty-five-year-old American captain and 6,000 pounds of tinned food, dried stockfish and medicines. I did almost all the flying as it turned out my captain had limited experience of C-47s, and, as well, he needed his sleep.

We staged around West Africa: the Portuguese island of Porto Santo off Madeira, Bissau, and Abidjan where we were caught in a severe rainstorm. The unpressurised C-47 was built for bad weather, but showed it was true to type with constant leaks around the windshield. On the final night sector to Uli via São Tomé, dodging flak and a Russian MiG jet fighter, another standard fault developed when the port oil cooler sprang a leak The pressure dropped and I had to shut down the engine.

haddock. © Steven G. Johnson.

Stockfish is central to my tale. It is unsalted cod, gutted, filleted and dried by cold air and wind for three months on wooden racks on Norwegian foreshores, centred on Lofoten. This way of doing things goes back to the Vikings. The stockfish is cured by fermentation in which bacteria matures the fish, similar to the process with cheese. The result is as hard as nails and dry as tree bark. It is rich in proteins, vitamins, iron and calcium. The smell is pungent and clings to the back of your throat.

Stockfish was also the lifesaver in Biafra.

I was staying on a small airfield at Uga, about thirty kilometres north-east of the main Uli airstrip. I set about trying to understand more about the famine

---

7 Heal, Chris, *Disappearing* (C&S 2019), Chapter 3.

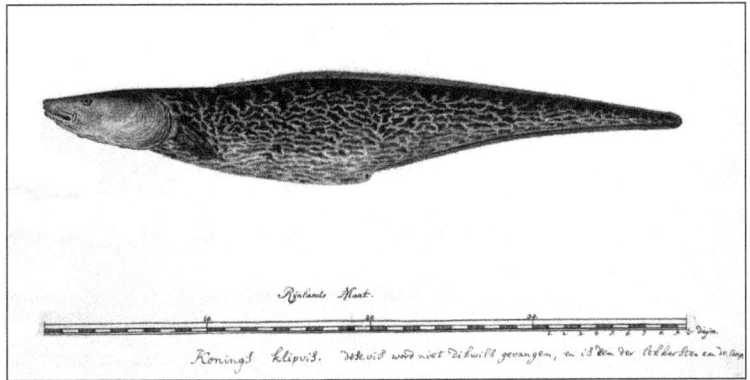

kingklip. ©Annals of the South African Museum.

that filled British newspapers and was, to my mind, why I was there. A stream of refugees trudged through carrying all they had.

There was no doubt that the average person was suffering from the rise in prices and shortages imposed by the British-led blockade. Beef had risen from three to sixty shillings a pound, but was seldom obtainable; eggs, once four shillings a dozen were thirty-eight; a chicken at perhaps fifteen shillings before the war rose first to £5, then £15; stockfish, the mainstay of the airlift, had gone from five shillings a pound to sixty; and, most dramatically, salt, once one penny a cup, was now twenty shillings. Rats, snails and mice all fetched a good price. Soap, cosmetics, most items of clothing and, of course, medicines were in short supply. Cigarettes and beer were unobtainable.

The priests and nuns noticed an increasing incidence of kwashiorkor, a disease which stems from protein deficiency and which mainly affects children. The symptoms are a reddening of the hair, paling of the skin, swelling of the joints and bloating of the flesh as it distends with water. The results were damage to the brain tissue, lethargy, coma and, finally, death. Besides kwashiorkor there was anaemia, pellagra, and just plain starvation, as children wasted away to skin and bone.

In the last days of June, the first pictures of small children reduced to living skeletons hit the pages of two London newspapers – *The Sun* and the *Daily Sketch*. Four hundred deaths a day spiralled to ten thousand. The Red Cross called it unequivocally 'the gravest emergency' it had handled since World War Two. The reporter and later author Frederick Forsyth, his personal disgust growing by the day, said, 'The most scabrous act of all was the British Government plus the American State Department during August and September attempting to interfere with relief by pressuring the Red Cross not to send any supplies at all.'

US president Richard Nixon called it genocide.

No one had foreseen the famine because no one thought the war would last this long. Extreme protein deficiency transformed an incompetent bush war into a massive humanitarian tragedy the like of which neither Africa, nor Europe, nor North America had even seen.

The children died in the villages, by the roadsides and, alongside those who survived on the relief food, in the feeding centres and, sad to say, there were two near us at Uga. They were built around the local missions, church, school, dispensary and a field the size of a football pitch where the wasted children lay on the grass, on rush mats or the laps of their mothers, who held them close, watching them wither and slip away. As the effects of kwashiorkor intensified, the dark brown curly hair diminished to a ginger fizz. The eyes lost focus, but appeared immense in the wizened face. The weakness of departed muscle made them listless until, unable to move at all, they died and a figure in a cassock came to intone a last blessing and take them to the pit.

For several weeks, I spent about two hours each morning digging these pits until my hands blistered and then helped to fill them.

When my time in Biafra was over, I left Uli one evening for Portugal. We made good time and I was able to have a late solo lunch in Faro with a bottle of *vinho verde*. About half way through, I had a quiet few minutes gazing into the distance. What I had ordered without thought was *bacalhau*, the classic Portuguese dish made with salted or dried cod.

The bitter irony is that for our one-time enemy, Nigeria, stockfish is now the great love affair for local cooking. After the civil war, stockfish became the must-have ingredient in Nigerian cuisine. Over two hundred containers are sent each year to take centre place in the country's teeming markets. It is perfect for the local palate which favours big and bold flavours, rich, intense and complex.

snoek.

flatfish by knife

dab, plaice, skate, turbot,

Of all the animals we eat, how many do we capture, kill and prepare ourselves? How close do we get today to the slaughter house?

Some animals we still buy live, like oysters, and eat them raw at the table, letting our stomachs do the work.

Some animals we might buy live, like clams, lobster, mussels or scallops, and then despatch them in the kitchen. If we live by the sea, we might include shore shellfish like razor fish, barnacles, cockles and small crabs.

For those few of us who have managed to hold on to a shotgun or rifle, we can shoot in the wild: game birds, woodpigeon, deer and rabbit, but not many would have the experience or stomach to know what to do next. Those who use a rod to fish rivers or sea might bring home any manner of carcass, sustainable species only of course. In rare cases, some animals like trout from a local lake farm may be ungutted and not portioned and plastic wrapped.

The days are long gone for most of us when we will wring a chicken or turkey's neck or bite the neck of a juicy rat.

For the great majority of what we eat, we rely on the sanitised shop or restaurant.

There is one group I have missed out and it is the subject of this chapter: those who are happy to use a knife, to get up close and personal. It is, or was in my case, the preserve of the amateur diver.

Over fifty years ago, I was holidaying with friends in Porthleven in Cornwall. Vacations in the 1970s meant going diving. That particular day, we drove

turbot. © Luc Viatour, https://Lucnix.be.

through Helston to Falmouth to find the wrecks of five World War One u-boats that were lying in shallow water near Pendennis Point.

Germany was required to hand over all of their serviceable u-boats as war reparations. Approaching two hundred vessels in a line five miles long gathered off Felixstowe in November 1918, later transferring to the River Stour at Harwich. The crews were all shipped back to their homeland without setting foot in England. Records at the time were unclear: some were rust buckets and were beached to rot, others were taken into the Royal Navy or transferred to Allied fleets, yet others were taken on a grand tour to show off the British victory, a large number seemed to sink under tow. Seven were sent to Falmouth to be used as experiments on how best to sink submarines in conflict; one, UB 118, foundered on the way and was sunk.[8]

In November 1920, seventeen trials took place over three weeks when different amounts of explosives were placed at varying distances and depths.[9] Further tests took place next year, finishing in March before what was left was hauled as near to shore as possible. Five of the u-boats were close together and were in quite a mess.

The British choice of u-boats to blow up was interesting. Apart from a mine-layer, all were Class III coastal torpedo boats, modern, launched after late 1917, and of a successful type. Their predecessors, the Class I, known as sewing machines, were highly dangerous and feeble as fighting ships.[10] Clandestine work had already begun in Germany on preparing for World War Two and the Class III design with an all-welded construction was the basis of that 1939 fleet.[11]

Today, at Falmouth these boats are so reduced as to be nothing more than a shallow training dive. We swam down five metres but found they were a tad boring. There was blast wreckage everywhere. Mottled cat sharks and large, brightly-coloured wrasse floated in and out of the kelp. I had just picked up a souvenir, what I called in jest a porthole, but was likely just an engine ring, when I spotted the outline of a pale brown flatfish on the sandy bottom. It was a common dab, about twelve inches, not the best tasting, but worth a catch.

---

8   McCartney, *Lost Patrols*, pp. 51–55. The Falmouth u-boats: UC 92, UB 86, UB 97, UB 106, UB 112 and UB 128, the boat of later Admiral Wilhelm Canaris, chief of the Abwehr from 1935.
9   Compare with similar tests on UC 61 at Wissant, south of Calais: Heal, Chris, *Sound of Hunger* (Unicorn 2018), pp. 383-84.
10 Heal, *Sound of Hunger*, pp. 214-15.
11 Heal, *Sound of Hunger*, pp. 527-28.

I unhitched my knife from my leg, swam up behind it slowly and stabbed it in the neck. Just as I was transferring the fish to my net bag a school of pilchards and their young sardines darted shining above.

We identified four of the u-boats, two so far up the beach they would have been visible from the shore at low tide.

common dab. © Hans Hillewaert.

Afterwards, as we climbed to the road we decided to go back to Porthleven with our second bottles for another dive around the west point of the harbour. It would mean driving out to a quiet spot and running our air compressor for a couple of hours that evening.

We hadn't been in the water for ten minutes and were hardly thirty metres out when I saw the familiar shape of another flatfish, bigger than the dab, much bigger. As a fish settles, it slowly flaps its fins so that the disturbed sand falls back to provide camouflage. It can take an experienced eye to see a slight outline on the sea floor. Out came the knife. I half expected a flash of wing as my spooked prey disappeared. As the blade went in, the large freckled fish rose, wriggled slightly and settled, dead. I had just caught a turbot, perhaps two thirds of a metre. It was so large that it would not fit in my net, so heavy that the best way to carry it was with the knife still in place acting as a handle. It meant the end of the dive.

My landlady was all but hysterical. Friends and local fishermen were called and hastened around to bear witness. No turbot had been caught in these waters for over ten years. The fish weighed eighteen kilograms. My landlady claimed half as cooking bounty. We had the white fillets basted in bubbling butter for dinner and for breakfast the next day. It was my first taste of turbot and it remains my supreme fish experience.

In 2025, Michelin-starred chef Tommy Banks of Yorkshire lamented that turbot had become too expensive.[12]

---

12 Wolfson, Daniel, 'King of fish loses its crown amid price rise', *The Daily Telegraph*, 2/6/2025.

'It's the king of the sea, a beautiful fish, but it's just not affordable any more. You can't put it on the menu.'

At 2025 prices, my turbot would cost Mr Banks a little over £300.

On the way home from Cornwall, I called in on family friends in Dover where I had arranged a dive with the local club. The club set me up deliberately. I was a qualified instructor, but was left slyly on the shore with a novice who had to be taught and shepherded through every move. The dive was dangerous and I wasn't warned. We went in by a pier and soon found ourselves dodging almost invisible strings of lost fishing lines, many with nasty hooks still attached.

However, we did get our moment of glory as the shape of another flatfish appeared. It took a while to make my trainee realise what he was seeing. I lent him my knife and showed him what to do. It was a plaice with its distinctive red spots. He struck home and swallowed most of his air in excitement. It was his first kill.

'Plaice' comes from the Anglo-French *plais* and, in turn, from the late Latin *platessa*, meaning flatfish, which originated from the Ancient Greek *platys* meaning 'broad'. Now you know!

The plaice was scarcely stowed when another showed which I netted for myself. I am always surprised how much better tasting a fish is straight from the sea, this one white, tender and subtle with little smell. Mine fed four that night, simply grilled with a black butter sauce.[13] Plaice is one of the most common fish in North German and Danish cuisine, often eaten as an open sandwich with *remoulade* sauce and lemon slices or just plain battered fish and chips.[14] I read that plaice grow less quickly these days and, through overfishing, are rarely older than six years against a possible forty.

common skate. © Des Colhoun.

A month later, back in Scotland, I crossed by car ferry from my home in Largs to the island of Great Cumbrae,

---

13 Black butter sauce: butter with chopped capers and parsley.
14 Classic French *remoulade* sauce served cold: mayonnaise to which are added gherkins, mixed herbs (perhaps tarragon, parsley, chives and chervil), capers, all finely minced, Dijon mustard, white wine vinegar and a very finely chopped anchovy fillet with salt and pepper.

just a ten minute crossing. Turning north around the head, I reached Skate Bay. In those days, I never heard of anyone diving there. If it was called Skate Bay, were there skate there?

Local fishermen said the fish were already rare, but fifty years ago were plentiful. Skate spend their entire life in one small area so, if fished all year round, entire populations could be wiped out. I also had heard (reflect: in those days before mobile phones and the Internet, for information one had to rely on conversation or, heaven forfend, books) that Scottish skate was one of the largest creatures in British waters. They were closely related to sharks, sharing common features such as a skeleton made out of cartilage and the absence of a swim bladder.

Skate feed on crustaceans and molluscs, powerful jaws easily crunching through shells. They also feed on fish, especially seabed flatfish such as dab and plaice, and are capable of catching mackerel, herring, pollock and dogfish whole.[15]

I had chosen a warm day because, rumour had it, the sun brought skate into shallower water for easier feeding. Against all the rules, I was diving on my own, something I often preferred, but it meant special attention to the state of the tide. The bay did not look promising: pretty, but flat and sweeping with few rock outcrops. There was no one around. With little anticipation, I finned out into calm, clear water, often just drifting using my snorkel, and for thirty minutes saw nothing. Then I spotted a large crab by one isolated rock and dropped five metres to pick it up.

The mood changed. As I reached the sand, a great section shifted almost imperceptibly. This was a seriously big flatfish. For a minute, I wasn't even sure where the head lay. I got my bearings, took out my knife, expelled all air and slowly settled. I struck.

It was the biggest creature I had ever encountered apart from a pod of harmless basking sharks.

It took off with me holding grimly to my knife and headed out to sea.

Let go? Lose my knife? Hang on? Could I slow my great suckings of precious air in the excitement? Hit the main current and get dragged out to God knows where? Bump into a submerged nuclear submarine from the Gare Loch?

---

15 britishseafishing.co.uk/common-skate.

european plaice. © Hans Hillewaert

My shoulder felt as if it would tear. Luckily, the fish, which seemed all around me, didn't twist or I would have lost. It just swam straight, but always deeper. I was at ten metres, twelve.

With little air left for any decompression, the skate finally slowed and gradually swung back to shore until I reached standing depth. Then it died. I staggered and pulled till I could get no further and sat exhausted in the shallows. There was no witness.

I had to butcher it where I was and cut off the two massive wings which I carried in turn up the beach.

I read during research today that, in 2013, the boat record for rod and line caught skate could have been broken when David Griffiths from Sarn, Powys, caught a 235lb skate off the coast of Oban in Scotland. The rules state that fish has to be weighed on land and this would have been a death sentence and so it was set free.

A fully grown skate of, perhaps, seventy years can have a wingspan of a metre and a half. My skate was comfortably wider than I was tall at slightly under a metre. At home, each wing weighed about forty-five kilograms which I was just able to get to the car boot. A restaurant meal might mean two hundred and fifty grams. I had enough skate flesh for over three hundred and fifty people. I made good money at the fishmonger, filled the freezer and gave many steaks away and ate the fish every other day for a month, poached, grilled, roasted, but almost always with a brown butter and caper sauce with lemon.[16] Delicious, at least for the first few weeks.

Today, over fifty years later, the common skate is one of the most endangered species in the world, classed as 'Critically Endangered' by the IUCN (International Union for the Conservation of Nature). The wild species is at an extremely high risk of extinction in the near future.

---

16 Brown butter sauce: as for black butter, but with lemon juice.

fresh water book party

signal crayfish, eider duck, pike, roach, tench

Hay-on-Wye is a market town on the Welsh border with England. With over twenty bookshops, it is the 'National Book Town of Wales'. From the popularity of the cheek by jowl collections of old books, an annual international literary festival grew drawing some eighty thousand people each early summer. Ironically, the Festival deals with new books and the vagaries of the publishing industry while the shops sell their remainders and their readers' unwanted second-hand books at lower prices. Hay is twinned with Timbuktu in Mali, famous as an Islamic centre of learning and for its private manuscript collections which I once visited.[17]

I was in Hay for two reasons.

The first was a fringe of the festival fringe meeting about accuracy in writing history books. In some views, I had overstepped the academic line when I had given a talk on the matter at the university in Winchester. The festival had a last minute cancellation and I was cajoled into the gap; arrogance winning the day, really. Twelve people turned up to hear my dressing down from an elderly professor from Oxford.

The nub of the argument was that my histories told stories about real people and included dialogue and attendance at events which could not be proved to have taken place.[18] These books were, therefore, more akin to a novel, no matter how likely were the facts they contained. A novel was the lowest form of human endeavour and unworthy of anyone with a doctorate. Grudgingly, the audience heard that I could write proper history books, but that only made my crime of factual misdemeanour more heinous.[19]

---

17 Heal, Chris, *Reappearing* (C&S 2020), chapters 2-3.
18 Heal, Chris, *The Winchester Tales*, (C&S 2022) & *The Four Marks Murders* (C&S 2021).
19 Heal, Chris, *Sound of Hunger* (Unicorn 2018) & *Ropley's Legacy* (C&S 2021).

signal crayfish. © Astacoides.

I based my defence on a book which sold well, *The Winchester Tales*, which dealt with the Norman invasion of the city in 1066 and the following theft of all Anglo-Saxon land. Over fifty per cent of England is today still held by Norman descendants.[20] I laid out my research for inspection. Thirty-two well documented events. Fifteen main characters, all verifiable and whose lives were reconstructed in detail. Every conversation built from original manuscripts, mostly legal documents and personal letters in Old French. None of my detail was actually challenged; it was just assumed to be made up because no one had done the research before.

As a dramatic metaphor for what I had written, I poured a large glass of red wine while on stage. This, I said, represented the full body of research in the book. I then drew a phial of vinegar from my pocket and transferred a single drop into the wine to represent my supposed inventions.

'What you are telling me,' I told my adversary, 'is that this whole glass of good wine now has no value because of the addition of a smidgeon of vinegar.' I drank deep and had to keep a happy face as it tasted foul. 'You are also saying that all the interpretation and conjecture in a normal history book is somehow academically acceptable and does not pollute the wine of history.'

I was accused of introducing confusing over-dramaticism. I gave up. I think I lost ten to two.

The second reason for visiting Hay was a little publicised and, therefore, little known food festival which was to follow the main literary event. The English / Welsh border running near the town is defined by the Dulas Brook, with numbers of contributing small streams, which joins the River Wye just to the north. Over the last twenty years this area had become the centre of

---

20 Cahill, Kevin, *Who owns Britain* (Canongate 2001), p. 22.

another invasion, not Norman but American. In the 1970s, the signal crayfish was introduced to be reared in water farms for restaurants and food shops. The crayfish escaped in large numbers, akin to the grey squirrel, and became established in the wild. It spread quickly throughout British rivers and streams and, today, holds the upper hand over the native species, the white-clawed crayfish, akin to the red squirrel.

More precisely, the signal crayfish is a cannibal and, if eating sister species doesn't achieve its ends, it passes on a crayfish plague through its numerous young. To complete the attack, signal crayfish burrow extensively into river banks eroding them. The area around Hay is a particular centre for these foreign forces.

It is the plain duty of all true English and Welsh gourmands to eat these critters in large numbers.

Of course, environmentalists are unhappy with this gastronomic solution, declaring that trapping for food in this case actually encourages population growth. This 'smash the gangs' approach has echoes of conversations about illegal crossings of the Bristol Channel. No doubt legislation to protect American crayfish in our best interests is on its way.

In the meantime, and happily, signal crayfish are very tasty.

From crayfish suppers grew the idea of promoting local fresh water fish. Eventually, four local pubs and restaurants banded to offer three days of products of the Hay streams.

On the first night, after the obligatory cracked crayfish with shallot, garlic and ginger, I had a roasted common eider duck, a large bird, the largest duck in Europe, that breeds all over the Atlantic and Arctic. The trouble is, as was carefully pointed out to me, the eider is not a fresh water animal but a seabird. Nature was still catching up with herself. Signal crayfish had become the bird's favoured treat and so the fresh waters around Hay had over the past twenty years become the

common male eider duck. © Ryzhkov Sergey.

new habitat of choice with a colony of over one thousand birds. The crayfish are swallowed whole, shells crushed in the gizzard and excreted. Eiders, which tend to return to their hatching sites, were now firmly established in the area. It was reckoned by those in the know that their meat was much less salty as a result. The bird's reputation had always been that of a 'trash duck'.

I went and chatted with the chef who was only too happy to share. The eider breasts were left to soak in brine for half the night, then they were pierced and left in milk till the next lunchtime. My host then marinaded them for three further hours in a secret concoction. The breasts were panfried in butter for three of four minutes on each side, then placed into a four hundred degree oven with a bacon covering for a further six minutes and left to rest for another three minutes before slicing. The big message was not to cook more than medium rare as the eider would dry and toughen quickly. Red wine, balsamic vinegar and sugar with a tad of water made a slightly tart sauce.

I thought it an excellent dish.

As a pleasant touch when I left, I was given a small cushion filled with eiderdown. These feathers used to be the height of luxury, but they now come free in Hay if you know where to look. They are taken from the nest lining when the ducklings have just left.

Next night, a different pub offered tench and the common roach.

Tench don't like the clear, rapid waters immediately around Hay, but prefer a muddier bottom with plenty of vegetation where the water has slowed to make a pool or join a lake. They have a carp-like shape with pretty olive-green skin above and almost golden below making them popular for ornamental ponds. Tench can get up to four kilograms although, that night, our chef had used two smaller fish to make into a smooth and mild-flavoured terrine. The fish was generously flaked with courgettes and thin peach slices into peppered ham aspic.

northern pike. © Jik jik.

Two medium-sized, silver-coloured roach provided the main course, served whole and grilled so that the skin had bubbled. They were placed on a bed of green rocket and warmed orange slices. Roach is another mild-flavoured fish with light, flaky flesh.

There was local apple tart to finish.

On the last night as I settled at my table, I had a surprise. My protagonist from the Festival debate arrived for the same

common roach. © Karelj.

sitting with what could only be his son. I waved, they came over and before I could shut my mouth I had invited them to join me.

'I'm pleased we have had this opportunity,' said the son, a little formally. 'I listened to your arguments and thought you were hard done by. The point you made about academic speculation being seen as somehow superior to dialogue compiled from solid research, was, I think, well made.'

'There is a precedent,' I offered. 'Orderic Vitalis in his history placed speeches into the mouths of the chief personalities in his stories in order to illustrate their character and policy. The work is, arguably, the greatest English social history of the Middle Ages.'[21]

The professor looked a little shifty in his seat as I spoke.

'I must add my own apology,' he said. 'I was a little arrogant. I had not read any of your books through, just skimmed then. I brought three with me intending to introduce arguments from them into the debate, but didn't find what I wanted. I've now read them thoroughly and, while not entirely convinced in some cases, I found the dialogue at least on a par with acceptable speculation.'

'In fact,' added the son, 'it seemed to me that the dialogue was of a higher intellectual quality than much speculation I have read. They can be two sides of the same coin.'

'Perhaps pike is an excellent choice for dinner,' I mused as the dish was brought on cue to the table. That brought a smile all around.

Pike is a notorious fighter especially when it is feeding. Cannibalism is never far away even among its own young because the fish's basic instincts

---

21 Vitalis, Orderic, *Historia Ecclesiastica*, eight volumes (1142); *The Winchester Tales*, p.183.

tench. © Karelj.

are instant and territorial. They are to be respected, often growing over a metre long and beyond twenty kilograms, and have sharp, backward-pointing teeth. Pike have been known to attack dogs, darting out of thick vegetation at speed. They are distinctive in catching prey sideways in the mouth, immobilising it, and then turning it headfirst before swallowing.

Our pike was served as a row of baked firm steaks, holding together well, with a stronger taste than other fresh water inhabitants. The steaks rested on a bed of pasta with a pesto sauce completed with diced tomatoes and crusty bread. I thought the pesto an excellent if surprising choice. The chef wandered over and he listed his ingredients: blended basil leaves, garlic and pine nuts, a drizzle of olive oil, a teaspoon of balsamic vinegar, then seasoning and a good dollop of Parmesan cheese.

The wine opened us up and, of course, we parted best of friends. Much of the meal was spent discussing my French sources found after lengthy research in Rouen.

Whenever I see a mention of the professor, I think of an older pike lying in ambush between water plants, perfectly still for many minutes, until the sudden flash and the careless death of one of its own offspring.

fruits de mer & jellied eels

clam, cockle, crab, spider crab, crevette, eel, krill, langoustine, mussel, oyster, periwinkle, prawn, shrimp, whelk

Where to start? Perhaps with the most satisfying lunch anywhere in the world?

If you are in the UK, leave. Take the overnight car ferry from Portsmouth to, say, Caen, and drive west along the Normandy coast. Visit the World War Two D-day cemeteries and realise how grateful you are to have the freedom to visit and eat in this part of the world.

Or try learning about another battle from another time at Bayeux. Its tapestry is an embroidered cloth nearly seventy metres long and fifty centimetre tall that depicts the events leading to the Norman Conquest of England in 1066, and culminating in the Battle of Hastings. It is now widely accepted to have been made in England, perhaps as a gift for William, England's newest king, and tells the story from the point of view of the conquerors.[22]

Then stop for a *fruits de mer*, 'fruits of the sea', lunch at St Aubin (Le Saint Aubin?), Courseulles-sur-Mer (Restaurant La Cremaillere?) or Arromanches (La Maison du 6?).

Decide whether to splash out for what may be a disappointingly chewy lobster (probably from Scotland and overcooked)? Or try a crab?

The royal choice would be a spider crab, a threatened species, but now commercially fished, two-thirds of the world catch from off the coast of France. The leg flesh is sweet and its orange carapace, up to twenty centimetres, has an abundance of white meat.

I remember introducing this animal to two young nieces in Concale in Brittany, famous for its expanse of inshore oyster beds feeding on the plankton

---

22 Heal, Chris, *The Winchester Tales* (C&S 2022).

fruits de mer.

of Mont-Saint-Michel Bay. The crab is ungainly and shocking to delicate minds with its long legs, in French *araignée de mer* for 'sea spider', but the promise of a large ice cream to come did the trick. Within a few grudging minutes of cracking shell and prising out the contents, they were converts. They still found room for their knee-high Knickerbocker glory.

Or choose an honest, cheaper, regular crab (imported from Cornwall?). Crab was standard weekly fare at my home in Largs in Scotland. In a good season, crab can be seen scuttling anywhere in shallow waters where they find rocks or kelp for cover if threatened. If you are diving, be careful to stay away from lines of crab pots. Fishermen are protective of their livings and may be unwelcoming.

My best crab dish came in a drop-in restaurant in Durban, South Africa: crab legs in a luscious curry sauce which brought tears of happiness. A close second was a similar dish at Rick Stein's in Winchester, but as they also served my worst ever *fruits de mer* (aged crab, a few cockles with dozens of mussels full of ice crystals and just a couple of oysters), I'll not publicise them.

I admit to a life-long craving for oysters. I've mentioned the oyster centre at Concale where freshness is a byword. In Paris, I once started dinner with a dozen each of *Fine de Claire* and *Utah Beach*. When it came to the main course, I balked at the many meat dishes and thought, 'Why not oysters?' Just a couple of dozen, including some *Plates*. I rounded the meal off with a dozen *rock* oysters. To their credit, not one hair was turned by the waiter.

Galway has an annual oyster festival, the local *rock* shells are small, but none the less tasty. Guiness is the preferred accompaniment. I sat in one of the many large tents near the shore, almost oystered out, when a gentlemen settled into a spare chair.

'Top of the morning.'

He chatted for a while, quickly recognised I was not Irish and moved on. I thought I recognised him. It was Michael Higgins, the man himself, president of free Ireland, born of the Cork Brigade of the Irish Republican Army, as always on the hunt for votes in his own constituency where he had also once been mayor.

One disappointment with your *fruits de mer* may be the mussels, but that's because you've sat already many times at an outside table in the main squares of Bruges or Ghent and eaten them, fat and succulent, straight from the cooking pot with fries and a cold something.

One measure of a good choice of *fruits de mer* is the variety of prawn included as standard.

The first among equals is langoustine, otherwise Dublin Bay prawn, Norway lobster or scampi. These are sweet and welcome mouthfuls, not a prawn at all but a small member of the lobster family and increasingly expensive. Fished from the north-west Atlantic, langoustine is Europe's most commercially important crustacean.

Then, perhaps, some version of tiger prawns, chewy and dependent entirely on their garlic sauce for taste, almost certainly farmed in chemical stews by sweated labour in Vietnam.

Smaller, but not by much, are the crevettes or king prawns, also heavily farmed in Asia. If you see wild catches advertised, take the opportunity. King prawns were the famous offering of a restaurant called Norman's in Johannesburg near to the rugby ground at Ellis Park. There was no menu. A

spider crab. © Govern de les Illes Balears.

grunted 'twelve', with a named sauce, garlic or mayonnaise, and 'yes' or 'no' to a salad to accompany the rice, was all that was required to place an order. Except that twelve was rarely enough. The shellfish used to come from fleets that operated off the Moçambique coast, but with the Communist take over by Frelimo in the 1980s the beds were sold to the Russians who cleared all stocks within two years. From then, there was a daily prawn Boeing 707 which flew from Australia to satisfy South Africa's appetite.

No self-respecting *fruits de mer* would be complete without a healthy scattering of shrimps, the sweetest of all. My favourite here is a small pot of these beasties caught off the beach at Southport in England, briefly boiled, seasoned and with the ramekin filled with parsley butter sauce and kept in the fridge to harden until dinner. A more recent and inferior alternative is krill, the food of basking sharks and others with large mouths who swim gaping and lazy. It's nearly impossible to skin these little krill to get to the pleasant flesh so what is there left to do but to take a mouthful, sucking the contents and spitting out the shells, a bit like taking the flesh from pomegranate seeds. It's not everyone's preferred way of eating.

Tucked away in corners of your plate are more little gems: sea snails like periwinkles, cooked in vinegar water and howked out with a pin, leaving only the hard plate of the foot to be discarded; and whelks, a much larger cousin of the same thing, brilliant eaten with mayonnaise. The meat of both is high in protein, omega-3 fatty acids and low in fat.

Razor shells and sea urchins are discussed elsewhere.[23] But, finally (hopefully) there is the sweet flesh of freshly cooked cockles and clams. I mention cockles again shortly. Clams, however, are never better found than in a *spaghetti vongole*, a dish so simple to make yet so perfect in flavour as to be one of the great culinary inventions. I nominate two small restaurants in Italy which may just have been having a very good day: the small bar at the public swimming pool in Ravello and a mountainside retreat come petrol station with a terrace view of the hills above Tremezzo on Lake Como.

And the wine? The options are endless: a Pinot Grigio from Venice? a Bourgogne Aligoté? Why not stay near the bottom of the *carte* with a Muscadet, but make sure it is *sur lie*, left to lie on the lees after fermentation to deepen the flavour. Perhaps two bottles? And a basket of just cut baguette

---

23 Chapter 'diving delights'.

… and mayonnaise … and red wine vinaigrette … fresh lemon halves …

If none of the above is to your particular taste or pocket, you might warm to the English *fruits de mer* in and around Southend-on-Sea. It's surprising that this land which so ignores its natural bounty, or swaps it with the French for quicker customs queues, has only this one area that really celebrates its fish. But, of course, the English taste is to fry in batter, add chips, douse in vinegar or, my particular favourite, stew in jelly.

jellied eels. © Footballbooks.

Jellied European eels became a staple when in the eighteenth century the River Thames was so filthy with excrement and industrial waste that the only fish to survive was the bottom-feeding eel. Chopped (shucked) eels were, and still are, boiled in a spiced stock, mostly vinegar, nutmeg and lemon, and then allowed to cool and set in its natural gelatinous liquid. It is usually served cold. Early London, especially the East End, was awash with cheap and nutritious eel, pie and mash houses. The pies began as eel pies, but over time were made with minced beef and onion. The liquor is the special part, made from eel gravy and heavily flavoured parsley sauce, preferably covered in white pepper.

This English *fruits de mer* is completed with offerings of cockles and whelks boiled in vinegared water, and eaten out of the shells with more vinegar, tomato sauce or mass mayonnaise. The experience sits neatly alongside that other great English national dish, fish and chips fried in batter with, you may have guessed, splashings of vinegar and lashings of salt.[24] With strong tea, of course. No Muscadet here.

In summer, there are many waterside stalls on the Essex coast with takeaway offerings in a polystyrene cup and a plastic fork and paper napkin. All year round, try Osborne's Cafe or The Old Peterboat, both in Old Leigh, or Wilkies Shellfish Bar or the Jellied Eel Café, both Southend-on-Sea. There are many others.

---

24 Chapter 'fish'n'chips'n'biafra'.

garden fare

crow, red deer, partridge, pheasant, quail, rabbit, squirrel, turkey, wood pigeon

Drizzle has hung around all day. From my study window, the grey-black clouds are too heavy and cannot be bothered to move. Everything drips, shrubs, gutters, trees. Drip, drip, drip.

There is a flash of white high in a lime tree. It moves, half hidden, along a leaf-covered branch, drops a level and another till it is only a metre above the ground. The bushy tail is not yet full grown, but is standing proud and providing good balance. Then it leaps, hits the grass smoothly and dashes through unmown wild wheat and long grass stalks full of yellow dandelion and dying narcissus. The youngster has already learned the narrow tramped path to a poplar tree. A climb and a jump across to a telephone wire and its pole on the other side of the lane, then a hop to a five metre run along an electricity cable, all visible from the front of the bungalow. Suddenly, it is out of sight.

It was a baby grey squirrel with white belly prominent. Within the minute, it is followed by an even smaller sibling. A new family has claimed the garden. Acorns, hazelnuts and walnuts are now as good as lost and will be buried beneath tufts of grass around the mossy lawn against a bad winter.

Native to North America, these squirrels are fun to watch, but a pest. Introduced into the UK in the nineteenth century, the species spread rapidly and is now the common squirrel. There are an estimated three million of them. They have all but destroyed the native red, stealing its food and transferring a deadly virus to which these grey incomers are immune.

I ate squirrel only once. It was in New York State in the USA on a holiday to see the brilliant colours of the trees in Fall. In late September, the whole wide landscape becomes a vivid kaleidoscope of fiery reds, purple, browns and yellows. One night's accommodation was in a false 'olde worlde' village inn up a forest track. Inside was well decorated, log-fire warm and welcoming. I quizzed the lady of the house on the squirrel pie.

'They're good,' she offered, 'but because they are small, don't forget that it's a rodent, they have very little edible meat, less than half a pound. We're overrun with them and while they're easy to shoot, it all takes time to prepare. It's fiddly to get the meat.

'Squirrel is a bit like rabbit, gamey and earthy flavours. Rabbit is like chicken breast, but squirrel is similar to chicken thighs.'

She was right. Squirrel made an interesting pie with just the right pastry, excellent in the surroundings with a strong Californian red, the meat lighter flavoured and more delicate than I expected.

At home, I mused at my window. A black carrion crow flopped to the ground, followed by three more, independent and stalking for insects, heads jabbing. Their collective name, 'murder', was appropriate as they tugged at the earthworms. Strident 'caws' announced success. I remembered the old adage to identify them from rooks, 'Crows are never in a crowd.' These crows shared the same lime tree as the squirrels, co-existing in a mass of twigs and broken branches.

From the *Corvus* family, we have rooks and crows in the garden and also jackdaws, jays and occasional ravens which fight for control of the high pine tops with the buzzards. It seems the buzzards are winning.

I also ate crow only once. It was unintended. I was in New Delhi, India, short of money and always on the hunt for cheaper restaurants in a city of cheap restaurants. This latest was a bit of a dive. I suppose a strong curry sauce can provide cover for anything, but the menu said 'chicken'. The meat was more pungent than I like and a bit chewy and dry, but not badly so, especially as I was hungry. Everyone else seemed happy.

Regular runs to the toilet were a fact of Delhi life, described as 'Delhi belly'. I went to the backyard which housed the evil-smelling shack. On

carrion crow. © Ian Kirk.

the way, in the heat I passed five men sitting in a circle on a concrete floor, chatting happily, surrounded by a small hill of ripped crow carcasses, the meat collected in a large tin basin, flies occasionally wafted away.

I stood for a while, watching. One of the men must have noticed my gradual enlightenment.

'Indian chicken,' he explained with a broad smile.

There is a family of idioms for 'eating crow': doing or saying something, then being publicly proved wrong and having to apologise, such as 'eating dirt' and 'eating one's hat'.

female red deer. © Sharp Photography.

To westerners at least, a crow has always been seen as distasteful food. The crow as a type of raven is one of the birds listed in *Leviticus* as being unfit for the table.[25]

The crow/raven was also a favoured banner of many Viking chieftains. Scavenging carrion eaters have a long association with the battlefield,

> *They left them behind to divide up the carrion, the dusky-plumed fowl, that darkened raven, horn-beaked and that hazel-feathered eagle, white behind it, enjoying the slain, the greedy war-hawk and that grey beast, the wolf in the wold. Nor was there a greater slaughter upon this island ever yet …*[26]

---

25 *Leviticus*, third book of the *Old Testament*, Chapter 11.
26 *Anglo-Saxon Chronicle*, 'The Battle of Brunanburh', 60-73.

brown quail. © Duncan Wright.

One evening, I challenged young family members to guess the number of animals that I had seen in the garden. The right answer was well over a hundred, but no one got above twenty.[27]

One of the answers was hare. It is common on the chalk uplands a short distance away across the dry ancient river bed now a rat run, but I have only seen one make the garden. I took aim, but decided against firing. Shortly afterwards in the local market, I saw one skinned and wrapped in plastic. I took it home to try. The smell was overwhelming bad and sour. The joint was discarded promptly. I'm glad I left my garden visitor alone.

We also get our share of game birds: crested guinea fowl and peacock from next door, red-legged partridge, pheasant, and quail from the nearby shoots. The last three are available in numbers from the local game shop in Alresford. Roasted partridge or pheasant is regularly on the table.

Apart from the usual farm strays (bull, chicken, goat, sheep, horse), in season we get red and roe deer, often young males ejected from small herds in the local wood. It was late evening when the security lights came on. Nonchalant as you like, a hind was eating the roses, just the flowers you understand, with a particular liking for yellows, my favourites. As usual, I found later, the red deer

---

27 Ant (many), aphid (greenfly, blackfly), badger, common pipistrelle bat, bee (many), blackbird, brambling, bull, bullfinch, bumble bee, butterfly (red admiral, holly blue, brimstone, meadow brown, coma, painted lady, peacock, large white), buzzard, cat, chaffinch, chicken, chiffchaff, cockroach, crested guinea fowl, crow, cranefly, cuckoo, deer (red, roe), dog (Alsatian, boxer, collie, cockapoo, labrador, retriever, spaniel, vizsla), dove, dragonfly, dunnock, earwig, fieldfare, fly (many), fox, frog, grasshopper, goat, goldcrest, greenfinch, gull (common, herring, large black-backed), hare, harvestman (daddy longlegs), hedgehog, hobby, hornet, horse, human, jackdaw, jay, kestrel, black and red kite, ladybird (two spot, seven spot, twenty-two spot), lynx, magpie, house martin, mole, moth (many), hawk moth, mouse (field, house), nightjar, nuthatch, owl (barn, tawny), red-legged partridge, peacock, pigeon (feral, wood), pheasant, quail, rabbit, rat, raven, redwing, robin, rook, sheep, shrew, silverfish, slug, snail, sparrow (hedge, tree), spider (many), grey squirrel, starling, swallow, swift, tit (blue, coal, great, long-tailed), thrush (song, mistle), tick, toad, tree creeper, vole, pied wagtail, wasp (many), woodlouse, woodpecker (European, green), woodworm, worm (common slow, earth), wren, yellowhammer (126).

had chewed and rubbed the white paper bark off several silver birches and the trees were in danger of dying.

How do you get rid of a red deer? It allowed me to stand next to it while it was busy; it was almost tame. I had a mad thought. I got a length of rope and placed a noose around its neck and led it to the car, passing the rope through the driver's window opening. I drove the car slowly about three kilometres to the local butcher's, the animal happily trotting alongside, and left it tied to the front door handle.

Two days later, I called in for meat supplies and noticed a tray of fresh, local venison cuts. I got a wink from the butcher. Perhaps he had recognised me from the security cameras? He gave me a cut price. Very tasty it was, too, grilled with a Merlot to hand.

It was that same year that I decided to try something different for Christmas. I know many people like turkey, but I am not a great fan, but then I also dislike the excess of the great feast itself: far more than I normally eat, cooling faster than I can get to it, too much fuss.

The garden abounds in rabbit and wood pigeon. I shot two of each a few days before the big day and made a joint pie with both meats cut in chunks and cooked with carrot, celery, garlic, onion and potato. I have a particular knowledge of historic rabbit keeping from my PhD thesis when I needed to know about the use of their fur in felt hat making.[28] I had also eaten rabbit before in Gozo, off Malta, when on holiday with a granddaughter. The meat was tender with many small bones, slow cooked in a rich dark wine sauce and we both enjoyed it; as usual like chicken but a touch more gamey. Likewise, I

common wood pigeon. © Tristan Ferne.

---

28 Heal, Chris, 'The Felt Hat Industry of Bristol and South Gloucestershire, 1530-1909', unpublished PhD thesis, Bristol University, 2012, eg: pp. 277-79, 299-300; also available for free download at the British Library's EThOS site, ethos.bl.uk, ID: THESIS00618690.

had tried pigeon breast with a white sauce in a local pub restaurant; I made a personal note to make sure the breasts' stubborn outer membrane was removed from the pale flesh before cooking. It was a good meat, delicate and firm.

I recommend the combination. Also, at a cost of just four cartridges, a little cheaper than a whole turkey.

guga hunt

gannet

Over the darkened sea,
Only the voice of a flying duck
Is visible –
In soft white.[29]

Sula Sgeir is one of the most remote islands in the British Isles lying about seventy kilometres north of Lewis. Its modern name is from the Old Norse *súla*, 'gannet' and *sker*, 'skerry', a small rocky island. *Sula Sgeir* is the summit of a submarine mountain, 'black and hostile', a speck in the North Atlantic less than a kilometre long and typically one hundred metres wide.[30] It is made of hard gneiss rock formed under high temperature and pressure, often banded into pinks, whites and greys. Erosion causes the bedrock to sheer into long flat pieces. The sea has created a series of interconnected caves and tunnels throughout the southern part of the island.

Approached by a trawler even on an average day, the turquoise kelp-laden swell is dangerous and landing hazardous. During big Atlantic storms, waves smother the island. A small automated solar-powered lighthouse on the south end, seventy-four metres high, gives an eighteen kilometre warning. The structure is regularly damaged in gales.

Today, there are also five bothies in reasonable repair for annual local visitors. Legend says *Sula Sgeir* was once inhabited by the recluse Saint Brianhull, or Brenhilda, the sister of Saint Ronan of Iona. She was reportedly found dead

---

29 Bashō, Matsuo, 'The Records of a Weather-exposed Skeleton', *The Narrow Road to the Deep North* (Penguin 1966; 1684), p. 60. The Japanese name of this place is Tsuki-no-wa.
30 Macfarlane, Robert, *The Old Ways* (Penguin 2012), pp. 119-123, 135-137.

with a cormorant's nest in her ribcage. Some describe that ruin as a temple, perhaps in her memory called *Taigh Beannaichte*, 'Blessed House'.

I go down

easy into the earth, rise
again to the wispy tuft
of a shag's nest under

my picked-clean ribs.[31]

Sula Sgeir has been designated an 'Important Bird Area' by BirdLife International for its black-legged kittiwakes, common guillemots, puffins and northern fulmars, but it is best known for its five thousand breeding pairs of northern gannets, known in Scotland as the solan goose and their young birds in Gaelic as *guga*.

It wasn't snow – it was birds. Gannets, thousands of white gannets and their white guano and their white feathers, on every ledge of every cliff, and the air above the boat filled with flying gannets: their stout nicotine-yellow necks, their stiff-winged glides.[32]

Northern gannets are large with yellowish heads, black-tipped wings and long bills. They are the largest seabirds in the North Atlantic with a wingspan of up to two metres. The biggest northern gannet colony, about seventy-five thousand pairs, is on the Bass Rock off Edinburgh. They hunt fish by diving into the sea from thirty metres, pursuing their prey underwater. The gannet's capacity for eating large amounts has led to its name becoming slang for somebody with a voracious appetite. Gannets are from the genus *Morus*, ancient Greek for 'stupid' because, when breeding, they show no fear allowing them to be killed easily. Usually, the female gannet lays only one chalky-blue egg.

Written history of *Sula Sgeir* goes back to the sixteenth century and very probably before. Men from the Ness district of Lewis sailed in small craft to

---

31 Wheatley, David, 'St Brenhilda On Sula Sgeir' (1970). See also Van Vliet, Karla, 'On Brenhilda of Sula Sgeir', *Acumen*.
32 Macfarlane, *The Old Ways*, p. 135.

northern gannet. © Andreas Trepte.

'fetche hame thair boatful of dry wild fowls'.[33] In 1797, a 'most venturous set of people, at the hazard of their lives, went there in an open six-oared boat without even the aid of a compass'.[34] The flesh of the young gannet or *guga* is still regarded as a delicacy in Ness. It was a popular meat in earlier times in Scotland.

The *guga* hunt continues today as a tradition of great local importance. It would be illegal, but for an annual licence from Scottish National Heritage which declares the killing sustainable.[35]

In August each year, ten Nessmen, or maybe a dozen, chosen by lottery, sail five hours by trawler to *Sula Sgeir* to kill two thousand young birds.[36]

Author Peter May describes a night landing,

> *Chicks puked on his feet as he stumbled across the rocks by the light of his torch, overturning nests and sending birds squawking off into the night. The tarpaulin hanging across the entrance to the black house had been*

---

33 Munro, Dean, *Suilskeray*, No 12 (1549).
34 McDonald, Donald, *Statistical Account of Scotland* (1797).
35 Wildlife and Countryside Act 1981.
36 'Adventure Sulisgeir' (1962) and 'The Guga Hunters of Ness' (last shown 2011), BBC documentaries.

> *weighted down by heavy boulders. He yanked it free and pushed his way inside. He could see the embers of the peat fire in the centre of the room glowing still in the dark and he could smell the sour perfume of human sweat, a pitch above the pervasive smell of peat smoke. He flashed his torch around the walls, cutting through the blue, smoky air, and saw the shapes of men hunched on mattresses all along the stone shelf. Several of them were already stirring.*[37]

The men live for two weeks in the same repaired bothies as their grandfathers. It is hard and dangerous work on the cliffs, often in challenging weather. Working in pairs, the men hang by ropes and pulleys to take the fledglings by the neck from their nests with a noose on a pole. The birds are then killed by a hit over the head. The Scottish Society for the Prevention of Cruelty to Animals describes the hunt as 'barbaric and inhumane' because it believes unnecessary suffering is caused by the several head blows sometimes needed. Each bird is gutted, plucked, scorched, salted and stacked in large circles ready for the trip home.

> *Once the guga-hunting party had departed from Sula Sgeir each year, the amputated wings of the dead gannets – four thousands wings from two thousand birds – were left lying on the summit., so that when the next big autumn storm came and the next big wind blew from the south or the west, thousands of these severed wings would lift from the surfaces of the island, such that it seemed, when seen from the sea, that the rock itself were trying to lift off in flight – an entire island rising into the air, like Swift's Laputa.*[38]

One morning, there was a sense of the unusual about my autumn holiday hotel in Portree, the capital of the Isle of Skye. I asked a waitress at breakfast what was amiss, but she averted her eyes and moved on quickly. As I finished my coffee, the manager sidled to my table.

'Do you know of the *guga*?' he asked.

'I do,' I replied, 'but I have never tasted one. It is on my list.'

---

37 May, Peter, *The Black House* (Quercus 2011), p. 453.
38 Macfarlane, *The Old Ways*, p. 178. Laputa is a flying island in Swift, Jonathan, *Gulliver's Travels* (1726).

He gave me a careful appraisal before sharing his news. His second chef, Hamish, was a man from Ness. His brother had been selected for the annual *guga* hunt and had just returned. By convention, the birds were divided amongst the hunters and those crowds of islanders waiting dockside. Any birds left over were sold to help offset the costs of the trip.

We came to the rub. Hamish had secured two *guga* from his brother and they had just arrived at the hotel. The delivery was something to be kept quiet because any excess killing might be seen as profiteering and lead to a reduction in the annual quota.

To cover his own costs, Hamish had offered to sell one of the birds to the hotel for £20. A small piece of smoked bird would be served, with a few traditional small and firm potatoes, as a second course at tomorrow's dinner.

The manager seemed to speak from the corner of his mouth.

'Only to valued and discerning guests, you understand, sir. The supplement will be £5. Discretion is requested.'

He switched to a direct, conspiratorial gaze.

'It's not everyone's cup of tea,' I was warned.

The following evening, hopefully, those guests deemed unsuitable did not notice that something peculiar was happening. The smell was still strong as the plates were brought quietly to the table. The whole bird had been rinsed and soaked for over a day to try to rid it of the overwhelming saltiness and then boiled for four hours with further regular changes of water.

The meat was tender, chopped into bite-sized chunks with a quarter inch of fat left attached. The flavour started like mackerel, a shade unclean and slightly decadent like a fresh-cut black truffle, but quicky filled the mouth with an intense salt and game flavour. I thought of holding my nose as I lifted my fork but felt it would offend anxious watching eyes. Perhaps tradition outweighed taste. If you don't like, say, hare, don't go there.

I had a bottle of single malt *Torabhaig* at the ready which I took liberally and neat between mouthfuls. It was not an even contest. In bed that night, I drank a litre of cool, fresh water and wished for more.

hippie trail

chicken, cockroach, goat, sheep

Isfahan in Iran, a major city of over two million people, is a giant crossroads, one route north from Tehran continues south, the other travels west and east. I was going east about a thousand kilometres around the south of Afghanistan to the border with Pakistan.

The fame of Isfahan with its grand boulevards, covered bridges, Persian-Muslim architecture, palaces, tiled mosques and minarets led to the proverb *Esfahān nesf-e-jahān ast*, 'Isfahan is half the world'. I was sorry to leave it all behind after just three days. There were many historical buildings, monuments, paintings and artifacts still undiscovered.

The problem was the state of the British economy. Travellers leaving the UK could only take legally about £56 with them in cash into non-sterling areas. Having hitchhiked and bussed across Europe and Turkey there was little money left until Pakistan when I would be able to access my traveller's cheques. This was before plastic credit cards were invented. Cash was king.

The bus to the border, near the town of Zahedan, would take a day or two, nobody was sure. Much could go wrong on a trip through endless salt dessert. It was scheduled to leave at six in the morning and we were under way by nine, luggage thrown unceremoniously on the roof. In 1968, this was no state-of-the-art modern city inter-bus. The seats were wooden and slatted, the backs strung with wire; goats and chickens filled the aisle; the driver uncommunicative with only one eye under a voluminous black turban. The windows were permanently open; indeed, they wouldn't close. The busted springs dealt noisily as best they could with the ruts, bumps and dead animals. I spent the trip husbanding my loaves of *Sangak* bread and two bottles of water while reading Edward FitzGerald's translation of a selection of quatrains by Omar Khayyam.[39]

The bus evaded the small city of Zahedan and drove to the border near Mirjaveh, the official crossing. The only serious building was a *Beau Geste* fort with an occasional wandering soldier dragging an automatic rifle. A scattering of clay buildings lay where they fell. Here, I was told, a bus would come from Pakistan. There was no timetable. I thought it was, perhaps forty degrees. I found shade by pressing against the fort wall. A stuttering heating condenser hung above me and I stood catching drops of cold water in my mouth. Sand burned through the soles of my shoes.

There were no food stalls. The few other people had all come prepared with packages of provisions, ready for an uncertain wait. Above one dark-eyed doorless hut a bold sign hung on one nail, 'Hotel Zahedan'. It had a hardened mud floor. For a few dinars, I dropped my sleeping bag, rucksack for a pillow, glad not to have to put up the tent. Geckos called to each other across the walls. I wondered what they would taste like.

I woke in the early hours to a noise like crunching gravel. The sapping heat had given way to a desert cold. My watch was gone from my wrist. I reached for my wallet and passport tucked inside my pants. Everything was intact. My eyes accustomed to the moonlight as I sat upright in shock.

Every inch of wall and ceiling, every inch of my sleeping bag, was taken by hissing black cockroaches. There had been no sign of them in the day, but now I knew why the room was so cheap. I grabbed my belongings and ran, brushing bodies from my clothing.

Outside was soft light. People lay around under thousands of stars. Some men were quietly at prayer. Through this rough camp, a trough snaked with slowly running water. My hunger hit me and I filled my mess tin pausing when a large green glob of spit floated past. A camel kneeling on front legs to drink sized me up and gave a deep grunt. I placed the tin on my stove to heat and went back to gather a few handfuls of my erstwhile sleeping partners and sat watching the white lines shoot through the heavens.

---

39 *Rubáiyát of Omar Khayyám*, translated Edward FitzGerald (1859), quatrains attributed to Omar Khayyam (1048–1131), dubbed the 'Astronomer Poet of Persia'.

There is only one black cockroach, the oriental. They come out of their cracks and sewers in the cool of the desert night. I now know they live on rotting food and faeces and transfer bacteria and viruses which spread dysentery.

I boiled the roaches until the chitin, or shell, was soft enough to be called crunchy. I wrapped them all in the last of my bread, itself now stale. The taste was bitter, oily, nutty with slightly acidic flavours. Not a place to go normally, but my catch filled a small hole in my tight stomach.

My bus to Quetta arrived at what used to be lunchtime the next day. Within half an hour the dozen passengers were aboard, the crew of three bad tempered, rude and looking for a fight.

The desert continued monotonous, uncaring, until our night stop in a deserted village. The driver went off to check and came back with his news.

'Don't drink from well. People all gone. Cholera.'

The trip took the whole of the next day. Part of the route took us through the very south of the border with Afghanistan which we crossed four times through unmanned posts, stop bars pointing skywards. This bus, if anything, was worse than the one before. I risked several hours on the roof despite the sun because of the cooling hot wind and I could stretch out. This was a journey for sadists.

Quetta, much smaller then but still surrounded by the majestic peaks of the Balochistan mountains, was an oasis compared to the days before. The city is famous for its orchards, producing a variety of fruits like apples, apricots, dates, peaches, pomegranates and cherries and every variety of nut.

My downstairs room with a multi-cushioned bed opened onto a green courtyard of grass and flowers with one recliner which I claimed. The mosquitoes were busy but there was a net for sleeping.

My meal that night was *sajji*, lamb served rarish on rice that is cooked inside the animal after marinating in salt and a few zingy spices. A large plate of fresh fruits followed. The next day, I had my first *dum pukht*. The aged mutton and vegetables were slow-cooked over a low flame in a heavy-bottomed clay pot that was sealed with dough. *Murree* beer was freely served in those days.

Next morning, I took a train to Lahore and slept in a luggage rack under a bare light bulb, sweat dripping onto the people below. My pocket knife was stolen. I also remember looking out of the window in the middle of the night and seeing a sign claiming that this station, wherever it was, was the hottest place in the world.

oriental cockroach. © Syrio.

Some months later, for the return trip to London, I foreswore southern Pakistan and travelled the northern route from the Valley of Peshawar through the Khyber Pass to Kabul in Afghanistan.

I didn't know it at the time, but I was moving to and fro along what became known as the hippie trail. I never saw many hippies, just young people exploring as cheaply as they could, some with a keen interest in hashish, eastern religion and beaches. Imagine, today, being able to travel overland from London to Bangkok without much political or military hindrance. It all came to an end in the 1970s. The Boeing 707 brought the first cheap long-distance flights. The real killer was the Islamic revolution in Iran which blocked the route, then the Soviets invaded Afghanistan, and everyone invaded Lebanon, and, of course, the Nepalese and Sri Lankans fought their own civil wars. Local people also grew tired of the constant stream of immature self-centred freeloaders.

The Khyber Pass, part of the ancient Silk Road, is as dramatic as its legends suggest. It is long, winding, glorious and without peer. So many armies, Cyrus, Darius the first, Alexander, Genghis Khan, the Moguls, the Achaemenid, Sassanid and Parthian empires, the British, Russians and Americans, have fought for its control. The pass allowed the spread of Greek influence eastward and the expansion of Buddhism westward.

In Peshawar as I waited for a ramshackle bus, I took mint tea in a small drinking shop. After a few minutes I was ushered through curtains at the rear to a room which held every imaginable weapon from down the ages. The area is known for its counterfeit arms industry making 'Khyber Pass copies' using local steel and blacksmiths' forges.

When the bus reached the small, scruffy town of *Landi Kotal*, a stone's throw from the border, I and everyone else had to pay a small tribute before being allowed off. Guns were freely carried. All travellers were warned not to wander any distance from the road into the barely controlled tribal area. Hillside forts and British monuments dotted the hillside. It was easy then to imagine a local tribesman, Shinwari or Afridi, with a long-range single-shot rifle behind his favourite rock waiting patiently for the unwary to leave the crowd.

A notice declared that a banyan tree had been placed under arrest by a drunken British officer named James Squid in 1898. It was the one tourist attraction.

Landi Kotal was the site of my most memorable meal concerning the humble chicken. I sat on a drinks crate before a large wood fire in a courtyard. There was a strong smell of resin. Several rows of spits carrying chicken carcasses were turned slowly and carefully by young boys. Ashes and herbs were sprinkled. As future scrawny meals wandered clucking and pecking in the dirt around my feet, prospects did not seem good. I was handed half a bird cleaved in front of me. There was far more fat than with an anaemic European variety, far more taste than all the carefully woven French sauces in the cook books, just a pile of flat blackened bread to pick from and a communal pot of spiced tomato sauce. All around towered the mountains, most still topped with glaring white snow. Heaven!

I ate my first goat meat a handful of desert kilometres to the west of Kabul on the road to Kandahar. A large white warehouse stood alone amongst the arid scrub. A dozen small whirlwinds played and turned dramatically. Nearby was an all but derelict shack with several Pashtuns squatting on their haunches. A whole goat was roasting and I was invited for a small fee to wait half an hour to join them. One of the men took me into the warehouse.

A complete S.E.5a aircraft, originally a single-seat World War One biplane fighter, decorated with RAF insignia from the 1920s, hung by wire from the ceiling. The machine guns were in place and looked ready to fire. Below were racks upon racks of uniforms, mostly British from a long-gone war. I was asked to push a finger through blood-stained bullet holes. Carefully stacked lines of Lee Enfield rifles with Martini Henry cartridge loaders looked straight out of the Zulu campaigns. A Russian section in one corner held a regiment's worth of AK-47s and box upon steel box of ammunition. One large clay pot contained officers' swords.

As I ate my piece of that outstanding goat, I wondered how to find a container lorry to take the warehouse contents back to London for sale in Carnaby Street. The uniforms alone would make my fortune.

among the icebergs

abalone, emperor penguin, seal, walrus, killer whale

It was an evening like no other.

In two days time I had a flight booked from New Zealand to Punta Arenas in Chile to make a connection to Antarctica. It was a little present to myself for a successful business year. While I waited, I decided on one other indulgence. An abalone farm on the coast at Gisborne on North Island had an arrangement with a local hotel. I was determined to try the shellfish fresh and not out of a supermarket tin so I booked in for two nights.

In New Zealand, abalone, a substantial mollusc, is called *pāua*. The highly polished inner shell is extremely popular as souvenirs with its striking blue, green, and purple iridescence, but it was the meat I craved.

Like all New Zealand shellfish, recreational harvesting does not require a permit. The daily limit is ten *pāua* per snorkeller; SCUBA is banned. No one may be in possession of more than twenty pāua or more than two and a half kilograms of meat. This is awkward when the right to harvest *pāua* can be granted legally under Māori customary rights.

An extensive global black market exists in abalone meat. Poaching is a major industry in New Zealand. Convictions have resulted in seizure of diving gear, boats, and motor vehicles and fines and in rare cases, imprisonment.

The three-storey hotel was set on a slight promontory on a breathtaking sweeping bay, isolated from other tourist and commercial development. The beach was gently sloping with the low tide mark a long way out. Signs warned walkers to be wary of rushing tides. I had a seat in a bay window in the small restaurant and looked out over an expanse of blue without shipping, surfers or vapour trails. By previous arrangement a man was allocated the second seat at my table. He nodded affably.

braised abalone. © Avlxyz.

His face had an unmistakable pallor, recognisable to those in the know. There was also, sadly, a slight sour smell that hung in the air. It's the same but different in its own way with people who have spent years down a coal mine or, the opposite, the ruddiness of a gamekeeper whose whole working life has been outdoors in sun and rain.

I looked directly into the man's eyes and knew. And, of course, he knew I knew.

'Have you been out long?' I asked.

'Eleven days and four hours,' he said. 'I've come for a holiday and to see some forgotten relatives.' He paused. 'Takes one to know one,' he added.

'Do you want to talk about it?' It seemed he did.

'I murdered my wife. Stabbed her in a fit a rage with a kitchen knife. I got ten years.'

He glanced up to see how I was taking this.

'You want to know more?'

I spread my hands in invitation.

'We were married fifteen years. The first few were OK, but then she changed. Maybe I changed, too. Nothing I did was right. I was a failure. She never stopped, 24/7. I felt myself getting smaller and smaller. There was something in her voice, a tone, a whine, that got right under my skin. I hated her and what she had done to me. She never accepted what she was doing. Wouldn't talk about it. Wouldn't take counselling. It was, of course, all my fault.

'One day I just snapped. I picked up a knife and it went straight into her heart. Her eyes looked startled and then glazed. It was all over in second.'

There was no pause, no hesitation. I thought he was making a speech that he had given many times before, perhaps, to social workers, the police, probation boards.

My young abalone arrived, marinated and gently cooked in garlic, butter and lemon. Some tastes almost stop your heart.

I'm having that, too,' he said. He looked out of the window. 'Look at those birds.'

Five minutes before, occasional flocks of gannet, skua and various gull had passed in orderly fashion intent on their routine ending to a satisfactory day. Now, the sky was a whirling mass as if each colony had intermingled and been driven mad.

'How much of the ten years did you do?'

'Well, there's the thing,' he said. 'You get a third off anyway for good behaviour. The government got into a panic with prison overcrowding and my minimum sentence was reduced by half. Then they panicked some more and, if there was thought to be no danger of someone repeating their crime, it came down to a third. There was no one else I wanted to kill. I was no serial murderer. I had already done a year and a half on remand waiting for my trial. One day, the governor turned up at my cell and told me I was free. I'd done an extra eighteen months.

'I had some money from the house. So, here I am.'

'Look at that sky,' I interrupted. What had been a bright summer evening had closed down in minutes to a yellow fog shot through with pink and black. It reminded me of the London smogs of my youth.

The owner was doing the rounds.

'How's it…?' he began then saw the changed sky for the first time.

'Oh, no. Good God.'

He stepped back and climbed on a chair.

'Ladies and gentlemen,' he shouted. 'This is an extreme and urgent emergency. We are about to experience a tsunami. We have perhaps five minutes before it hits. If you go to your cars you will not

emperor penguins. © Ian Duffy.

be able to get away in time. The land around is all flat. You will not survive. This hotel is built for earthquake shocks. I ask you all to go to the top floor immediately. I will be switching off all power. You don't have time to get belongings. I suggest you place your passport, wallet, ID, in your underwear for safekeeping and to keep your hands free.'

'That'll make it easier to identify the bodies,' murmured my companion as we made for the stairs. There were about twenty people. Within minutes we were joined by three dogs, two ponies and a pair of hamsters.

I helped two elderly women make the climb, then stopped and looked over my shoulder.

Where there had been ocean there was now just a sea of flat sand with the occasional rock and a few wrecks of what seemed to be small pleasure boats. I went back and picked up my plate and a fork. Who knew when or if I would eat abalone again?

A small group gathered at my bedroom window. Jaws dropped in awe and fear. One moment no water could be seen and then a single wave moved in. There was no drama, no crashing seas, just a steady, rapid, inexorable rise of a smooth sea. I reached for my bottle of malt whisky, poured a few measures for others and drank straight from the bottle. From next door came the noise of a bed thumping against the wall followed by heartfelt moaning. Some guests had decided not to watch, but to spend their time another way.

The water reached the beach road, crossed it in a second, mounted the garden and its flowered paths, swallowed the front car park and climbed the hotel entrance steps. In a blink, half the lower windows disappeared. The building seemed to be floating.

Then the tsunami seemed to shudder and stopped.

We waited for, what, five long seconds and the sea slipped away down to the beach and past the low tide mark, turned and came again, only this time it paused a foot or two lower. As it fell back the second time, cars floated with it out to sea, some dead sheep, large trees, small boats and, I thought, a few human bodies. It was more graceful than turbulent.

Within ten minutes, the fog lifted, the dying sun played on blue water, birds resumed their flights and all was, almost, as it had been before.

I thanked everyone for their company and went to bed. In the morning, I gave the owner my credit card number in place of payment as there was no power. The water had reached a metre above the dining room floor and most of

orcas, killer whales. © Robert Pittman.

the furniture was stacked messily against the outside wall. I found my car in the upper park. It started first time, untouched by the wave. The drive to Auckland took eight hours with a long stop for breakfast. The radio told me that there had been an underwater earthquake or landslide way out in the South Pacific. A few isolated islands were all but destroyed., At least a thousand people were feared lost, but communications were bad everywhere. The total could be much more.

Two days later, I landed on King George Island in the South Shetlands. I was driven past Chile's 'Frei Station' and Russia's 'Bellingshausen Station', to a Zodiac inflatable which took me to a floating hotel. It was then that I started shaking, the last few days catching up. I hid in my cabin for twenty-four hours until I had control again.

When we reached the mainland, an endless blanket of snow, I looked to jump ship. I quickly found a small American scientific centre that gave me what I wanted: time and space to slow down and think. I joined the work crews, helped service the sledges, trekked out on glaciers to lay and check instruments, helped out in the kitchen.

The pantry was stocked high with tins, *Coca-Cola* and chocolate ice cream, but I had landed by chance with hunters. One freezer was still full of an orca, the black and white killer whale, that had been killed by the supply ship's propellors. The orca tasted like lean beef. Another freezer contained a walrus that had attacked and badly injured a young scientist and had been shot (deeply rich, slightly salty and sweet, different from all other meats, perhaps reflecting the animal's diet of clams and shellfish). For fresh meat, the hunters shot seal (really gamey and not my cup of tea) and emperor penguin, the tallest and heaviest of the species, (dark red meat, full of fat, tasting of fish and krill, their natural diet).

I stayed for three weeks and developed a taste for penguin. There was always a debate about whether it was legal or ethical to eat them, but then there were so many of them and so few were taken.

island love affairs

armadillo, conch, kipper, mahi-mahi, rabbitfish, seabream, red snapper, bigeye tuna, turtle, unknown fish

Which faraway place did you dream of visiting when you were a child? in my young teens, I was always travelling on a postal and supply steamer to islands in the Atlantic: the Azores, Cape Verde, Ascension Island, St Helena, Tristan da Cunha. A steamer left Bristol twice a year for the last three which were British islands. I was so besotted that as a ten-year-old I hitchhiked to the docks to see the Royal Mail Ship *St Helena* slip shore. I found out from the friendly purser whom I met at the bottom of the gangway that there were a handful of cabins for passengers. I started to save my pennies. I also had a piggy bank for getting to China.

It took me until I was over fifty to finally reach Ascension Island. There's not a lot there. It's an isolated volcanic place, just under ninety square kilometres, south of the equator, and over one a half thousand kilometres from the coast of Africa.

After days cramped in a small vessel what I wanted to do was stride out in the sun. I rejected walking the road up from the jetty to the small settlement. Instead I chose a steep incline of an old lava flow. The arid ground was orange cinder with grey chunks of clinker, devoid of anything green. There were no trees, no shade. It was thirty degrees and very hard work. After an hour, my second bottle of water finished, I began to think I had bitten off more than I sensibly should.

I reached a plateau with a few struggling shrubs among the stone pathways to find a man sitting on a boulder with a pair of binoculars. He looked like the sort of person who did triathlons in his sleep.

'Mad are you?' he said. It wasn't really a question. 'I've been watching you in case you needed rescuing.'

nine-banded armadillo. © www.birdphotos.com.

'Needed a bit of a workout,' I offered.

'I know what you need,' he said. 'A couple of beers.' He pointed to a large hut a hundred metres away. 'That's our canteen. Try the fish cakes.'

I sat at a trestle table, second large bottle of beer close by and ate my second helping of the best, cheapest fish cakes ever. The flavours were complex, the crumbs light and spiced.

I started looking around: an RAF sign pointed to the rubble of what might one day be a runway, a European Space Agency tracking station sported two white dishes alongside a largish building that belonged to a British-American signals intelligence facility, the BBC had a World Service Atlantic Relay Station and, then, a little tucked away a collection of small unfriendly buildings, one emblazoned with 'Who Dares Wins'. Everywhere else was the ocean.

A woman came from the canteen to collect my plate. I complimented her on the fish cakes.

'Made them myself, recipe handed down the generations.' She smiled. 'It's the soap from the washing up that does it.'

'And the fish?'

'Seabream. Gilt head. Fresh from the sea. My husband catches them by line. We sometimes get fed up just grilling them plain.'

I thought back to the gilt-head supermarket bream at home and the days before when it was a great meal, the gold band between the eyes signalling quality. I had almost stopped eating the fish. Writing this, I checked the internet: wild bream in the UK are mostly from the Mediterranean and are descendants of escaped farmed fish; just eight thousand tons a year, while the crowded Turkish and Greek farms produce one hundred and fifty thousand tons. Today, you have little chance of finding the real deal. It was the Germans' fault when they snapped up the local cottage industries for a song when the Greek economy was impoverished by the European Union in 2015.

Today, the big challenge for the gilt-head seabream farmers is skeletal abnormalities in their crop. This is mostly caused by high stocking densities during larval rearing, but also by parasitic infection which can destroy entire lagoons.

Some one thousand three hundred kilometres later I was on the island of St Helena, Napolean's death place and I visited his original grave. I also saw the world's longest-lived land mammal, a tortoise named Jonathan, reputed today to be one hundred and ninety-four years. There were lemurs in the trees but no unusual food to report.

The West Indian islands always provide something different.

In Tobago, I heard a rumour of an unusual dish, stewed armadillo. I was a little wary. I knew armadillo was a popular ingredient in Central and South America where the animal's hard back was used to make an Andean lute, the *charango*. What I had also heard was that the armadillo was often used in the study of leprosy. I had been to a leprosy camp and it is one of those images that stays with you forever. Armadillos have very low body temperatures which makes them hospitable to the leprosy bacterium that spreads throughout their bodies. The bacterium can be passed to humans through handing or eating armadillo flesh; ironic because the evidence shows that it was the Spanish conquistador incursion into the New World which infected the animal, and the Incas, in the first place.

Directions to the 'restaurant' didn't inspire confidence, especially at night. The place was twenty minutes up a minor mountain road until a sign pointed to a quarry. The building was set back in a far corner, a shack of corrugated iron with upturned bottle crates and wall benches for seats. There was no door. The tables were covered

queen conch. © Daniel Neal.

in plastic cloth. Lighting came from Kerosene lamps. The stew bubbled softly in an open pot hanging on a hook over wood logs. It looked best to give the cutlery a good wipe. Fellow clients were locals who shared a flagon of fire water which they drank with a bottle of beer.

It was all unexpectedly good, even the drink. I rate armadillo meat highly. The stew was served with rice, okra and callaloo, which can be any green leaf, but this I thought was spinach. The meat was cubed and included the shell, each piece with a gorgeous outer layer of fat. The taste was the usual chicken come pork come gamey, but really it is a flavour all of its own. I think the all-in cost was £10 at today's prices. Delicious.

On an island like Nevis, one might expect a shortage of meat rather than fish. Apart from the luxury hotels, which in those days were few, it was basic fresh fish dishes that were scarce. It was almost my last day there when I finally found what I was looking for while walking the beach late in the morning: today's catch laid out under the palms for choice, open fire, grilling only, no finesse, cold beer, ramshackle furniture, absolute bliss.

I chose a northern red snapper with light colouring, middle size, about half a metre long. I was told it was line caught with squid bait that morning off a local wreck. It was plonked on the table, its skin black bubbled and showing thin charcoal lines, with rice and salad eaten with a choice of fork or chop sticks and number of hot pickles. Firm, sweet, not fishy. Top dish.

Conch, that's the one with large decorative spiral shell that looks good on the bath rim at home, is actually a sea snail. They're harvested all around the Caribbean, but I had my first taste on Antigua where it's called *lambi*. It comes raw in salad, marinated in lime juice, olive oil, vinegar, garlic, green peppers and onions. It can also be used in curries or fried in burgers or fritters. It's a good flavour and much lighter than the snails used in French cooking.

Conch shells are used as wind instruments with a hole cut in the spire near the apex and then blown like a trumpet. Fishermen on the island blast the shell to announce when their market is open.

Beware, though. In the UK, conch shells are an illegal import, the ninth most seized item taken by the customs men.

The Seychelles, the smallest country in Africa, has over one hundred and fifty islands and a population of a little over one hundred thousand people, an eclectic mix of French, British and slaves from Africa with infusions of Chinese and Indians. None of its people are indigenous; it was empty when the Europeans arrived and stayed a British colony from 1814 until independence in 1976. Mahé, its largest island, is also home to the Seychelloise capital, Victoria, which is where I was dropped for just twelve hours.

mahi-mahi. © Citron.

I drank an early morning beer in a main street café, admired the red telephone box, the statuary and the light traffic and visited the market. The island was reputedly a beautiful place so the best thing to do to fill my time before finding my boat was to hire a car and make a circumnavigation, stopping for beach, lunch and any curiosities on the way. The route was just over ninety kilometres, three hours going non-stop, but who was going to do that on this steep and winding road. Each beach had a rutted track to a white paradise with a drinks shack at one end under the palms.

To the south, up in the hills, a small sign suggested lunch. The tables were set on a veranda open on three sides to the breeze and views of the blue ocean. There was no one else there. All that was on offer was a choice from three fish caught that morning: I decided to try all of them and waited patiently with beer and a plate of fresh fruit. One was dolphin or dorado, not the real dolphin or dorado, but mahi-mahi. The distinguishing feature on this male is a protruding forehead, a lump really, showing against dazzling blues and greens and golden sides. Eat mahi-mahi when it is fresh; toxic bacteria grow when it is poorly kept. The second was rabbitfish with its venomous spines which I identified later from the market. Some species are reported hallucinogenic. Finally, there was a fish which I have never identified, which is a shame because, while the first two were excellent, this was in a royal league.

This 'royal unknown' stands for me for all the anonymous fish I have eaten and to whose name I wish I had paid more attention at the time. Taken together, I estimate my total of devoured species would swim well pass the current 0.002 per cent of what might be possible were I to live long enough.

All three of my Seychelles fish were served lightly grilled with salad and lemon on the side. The dessert, to my surprise, was crème brûlée.

I don't know if you have read Ernest Hemingway's *The Old Man and the Sea*, a short story and his last major fictional work. It tells of Santiago, an ageing fisherman, and his long struggle to catch a giant marlin.[40]

That morning, fifty odd years ago, the story flooded back as I found a large bigeye tuna pulled ashore by local fisherman in great excitement on a beach on the island of Grande Comore, mid-way between Madagascar and Moçambique. The catch was about fifty metres from my thatched hut in a small collection of well-separated buildings, mostly occupied by French holidaymakers. Near my door ran a river of black and just cooled lava from a recent eruption. The air was full of the sea and scents from vanilla vines with their long pods and the cananga tree which produces flowers that distil to make ylang-ylang, the basis for most perfumes. The day before in the capital, Moroni, I called by chance into a drinking den set among wild guava trees covered in fruit bats the size of monkeys. At the bar was an old diving buddy last seen ten years before on the Scottish coast.

The family that owned my hut acquired most of the tuna from the fisherman, one of their casual employees. He had caught it by line and speared it reluctantly as he was tiring more quickly than the fish and because blood would likely bring the sharks. This tuna's big eye enabled it to dive deep and to see well in low light conditions up to half a kilometre below. It was over two metres long; the chef's knives were already well at work.

It was the sweetest, lightest tuna I have ever eaten only outdone by bluefin tuna used in *sushi* in Tokyo.[41]

There was a problem, however. My son had recently declared that he did not like fish. Any fish. I had a short conversation with the waiter and arranged a dish of veal steak, suitably covered with potatoes and sauce so that it looked nothing like tuna. My son said his meal was delicious, too.

My favourite island is Sri Lanka. My favourite hotel is *The Last House* near Tangalle on the south coast. The tourist website barely does it justice, 'On one of Sri Lanka's most secluded castaway beaches, two kilometres long … a two-storey seaside villa … most magical haven … pillared verandas … rooms cooled by ocean breezes … laze in a roll top bath and watch the sun go down.'[42] The food is excellent.

---

40 See later chapter 'retribution'.
41 See later chapter 'sushi paradise'.
42 www.srilankacollection.com.

At the other end of the beach is a small fishing village which I walked to each early morning. There was an exhilaration mirroring that day when the bigeye tuna was brought ashore on the Comoros. This time it was a very large loggerhead turtle. It had been caught in a seine net and by the time it was found had drowned.

I knew the loggerhead well from time in Oman which has the animal's largest nesting site in the Indian Ocean – some fifteen thousand. I had eaten turtle eggs, a local delicacy, and even watched the turtles lay their eggs by inelegantly lifting a flipper as they dropped into a pre-dug hole, but I had never eaten the animal.

The loggerhead is the world's largest hard-shelled turtle. This one had a red shell with a yellowish skin. They roam the world. I have seen them underwater in several places. At night, they sleep with their eyes tight shut and and wake slowly, staying submerged for up to four hours. They can live to be over sixty. Their biggest killer seems to be plastic waste and abandoned fishing lines.

I arrived at the village as the turtle was being loaded into a lorry. I had to barter hard to make sure some of the meat was delivered to my hotel. I think I paid well over the price, but was surprised that afternoon to find I had bought the large carapace as well. I am told it now hangs on the wall in the reception.

I had to fight to make sure that, as with everything else in Sri Lanka, it was not curried. The taste was rich and buttery, sweet and nutty, a connoisseur's dish to savour, perhaps near to crawfish or lobster with firm and flaky flesh.

After several exotic locations, it may seem strange to end my island visits back in Scotland. I stayed at a well-to-do bed and breakfast on Mull, the place where the evening midges come in tens of thousands and are each large enough to eat a horse. After a substantial dinner, this place served an even more substantial 'tea' at nine in the evening after a visit to the pub. I never thought I would have room to eat again.

But, the next morning, I had the most succulent pair of kippers, sweet,

rabbitfish. © Leonard Low.

dripping oil, meaty, just outright delicious. Kippers are the kings of the herring products, split butterfly fashion, gutted, salted and cold-smoked over oak chips. Bloaters are herrings cold-smoked whole while bucklings are hot-smoked whole. I had tried both in Great Yarmouth.

The greatest treat is kipper, 'red herrings', eaten with bread and butter for dinner with an accompanying glass or two of whisky.

sushi paradise

carp, wagyu cow, cuttlefish, bluefin tuna, minke whale

What sets Japanese food apart is its consistent quality especially if you are prepared to pay for it. Ten years ago, staying at a high end hotel in Tokyo, I ordered two cups of tea in dinky porcelain and two highly-recommended small cakes, perhaps a bite and a half's worth. Excellent, but blink and it's gone. I made an acerbic comment at reception when shown the bill for over £40.

'The best comes at a price, sir.'

That's not to say that eating out is always pricey in Japan, far from it, but perhaps that little tale will act as a warning.

Wagyu beef is among the most expensive meats in the world. The rarest steak can cost over £250. Wagyu is the collective name for the four principal Japanese breeds that originated from crossing native Japanese cattle and, mostly, imported European stock. The story is long and interesting but given here in a much reduced explanation. Until the middle of the nineteenth century, cattle were used only as draught animals in mining, farming and transport and for fertiliser. Drinking milk and eating beef was unknown for cultural and religious reasons.

In 1859, Japan, a previously closed society, opened the port of Yokohama, followed by Kobe, after threats from many European nations demanding access to free trade. Kobe black beef was crossed with imports and a legend grew.

'There never has been beef as good as Kobe's beef.'[43]

One of the primary characteristics of Wagyu beef is the fine marbling of fat within the red meat, called *sashi*, which only occurs with the black beef crosses. *Sashi* is rich in monounsaturated fatty acids which have a melting point of around thirty degrees Celsius, below that of butter. Normally, the melting point

---

43 Nōbi, Shigeyoshi, *Flowers of Kobe* (1897), p. 90.

of beef fat is forty to fifty degrees Celsius. Wagyu beef fat melts as soon as it is put in the mouth and, it is thought, is one of the main reasons for the tender texture. Black beef also contains complex compounds of lactones, also found in peaches and coconuts, which give off heightened aromas when heated.

I had my first Wagyu steak, barely cooked, in a funny little restaurant high in a skyscraper. It was served without a knife; slices were cut with the side of the fork. It did melt almost as soon as it entered the mouth. A sweet smell followed and lingered. Nothing was chewed. Without doubt, it was the best steak I have even swallowed, but would I choose it over a beef steak cooked above the embers of a dying log fire?

The rest of this short chapter is about *sushi*, the one luxury that will accompany me to my desert island, the food that I could eat every day and, in Japan, probably did. I have tried *sushi* the world over and seldom found a taste and quality to match the best esteemed in its homeland. In fact, if you have only had *sushi* in the UK, even from a specialist shop, you don't know what you are missing.

Wagyu may be top of the Japanese money tree but, in my experience, it is beaten for taste by *sushi* royalty, the bluefin tuna. I've written in this book of bigeye tuna (Grande Comore) and yellowfin tuna (London), but there is no doubt about which kind is pre-eminent.[44] There are close similarities, marbling and price, with Wagyu beef.

japanese carp. © Mark Doliner.

Evenly distributed fat gives the bluefin tuna meat a velvety texture and rich flavour; the *otoro* at the bottom of the belly of the Atlantic and Pacific varieties is the prized cut. At the 2019 New Year auction in Tokyo's *Tsukiji* fish market, a two hundred and eighty kilogram Pacific bluefin was bought for a record $3.1 million by the

---

44 Chapters 'island love affairs' and 'lucky restaurants'.

owner of a popular *sushi* chain. This was extreme, but tuna over two hundred kilograms can cost over $100,000. *Otoro* belly pieces intended for *sushi*, sold in two kilogram cuts, can each go for several hundred dollars.

I sat at the bar having first eaten a few pieces of yellowfin tuna for comparison. My selection was served with reverence and the chefs gathered to judge my reaction.

highest grade wagyu beef. © Schellack.

It wasn't at all fishy, but slightly sweet, meaty, buttery and fatty. The overall taste was exquisite. It is the sort of preparation where, if you can, you forget the price and embrace heaven. Smaller bites mean the piece can be savoured for longer.

As a show off, the chefs prepared the smallest *sushi*, a line of offerings, each perhaps three millimetres long. The flavour still shone through.

There is one other taste with bluefin, left till now so as not to put anyone off. *Umami* is one of the five basic flavours of Japanese food, characteristic of broths and cooked meats. Foods that have a strong *umami* flavour include meats, shellfish, fish, tomatoes, mushrooms, meat extract, cheeses and soy sauce. In 1908, Dr Kikunae Ikeda of the University of Tokyo identified *umami* as a distinct taste attributed to glutamic acid. As a result, Ikeda and colleague Saburōsuke Suzuki founded the Ajinomoto Company which introduced the world's first *umami* seasoning: monosodium glutamate (MSG). MSG subsequently spread worldwide as a seasoning capable of enhancing *umami* in a wide variety of dishes.

MSG got its worst Press when its effects were called 'Chinese Restaurant Syndrome': a collection of complaints such as headache, nausea and a strange numbness after eating. Following years of tests, the jury is still out.

Japan was notorious in the twentieth century, and long before, for its determination to kill whales for meat and for oil. A whaling ship or land station could be smelled while out of sight and some distance from shore, similar to the stench of slave ships arriving from the West Indies with sugar at, say, Liverpool. This smell combined with the stories of docile mammals harpooned while

giant cuttlefish. © Ben Jobson.

lazing on the surface did much to turn the public's perception away from the practice.

Whale oil, or train-oil, is obtained by boiling strips of blubber cut in strips from the harvested animals, usually baleen whales. The removal is known as 'flensing'; the boiling process was called 'trying out'. The boiling is carried out on land when whales were caught close to shore and beached. On longer, deep-sea whaling expeditions, the trying-out was done in a furnace aboard the ship. The carcass was then discarded into the water.

This hunting reached a peak in Japan after the second world war and until 1960 when protein was in short supply. The country's catch limit for whales today is three hundred and eighty-three, mostly minke whales. Fleets are no longer allowed to roam the seas, but must stay within territorial waters. This level of consumption is akin to the decline of the French preference for horse.[45] Whale is mostly eaten by the older generation remembering their childhood. With Japan, only Iceland and Norway continue the hunt.

Tokyo offers a couple of 'one product' whale restaurants and they are still well frequented.

I had my chance at an exotic *sushi* bar in a Tokyo suburb. Rather than a *wasabi* horseradish smear, these slices of whale meat came coated with ginger. I was told this was to cut through the slightly greasy texture. Pushed to describe the flavour, I would say it was a cross between seared tuna and a ribeye steak. I had two pieces, but quickly reverted to fish and shellfish options.

My exotic *sushi* bar restaurant offered me two other firsts: carp and cuttlefish.

Carp is prized in the Old World, but they are considered trash fish and invasive pests in many parts of Africa, Australia and most of the United States. Some species are able to survive for months with practically no oxygen, for instance under ice or in stagnant, scummy water. Views varied. For instance,

---

45 Chapter 'out of africa'.

in 1653, Izaak Walton, wrote in *The Compleat Angler*, 'The carp is the queen of the rivers; a stately, a good, and a very subtle fish that was not at first bred, nor hath been long in England. But it is now naturalised.'

The Japanese agree with Walton and esteem carp for its delicate flavour. In their clear ponds they take great effort to disassociate it from its 'stagnant' reputation. Carp, from fair ground goldfish to ornamental koi, is regularly seen in careful gardens with the right selection of cleansing vegetation. I ate the fish in two dishes: thick *miso* soup with carp and as *sushi*. They are heavily boned so take care away from the fastidious restaurants. The flavour is tender, flaky and delicate and needs little *wasabi*. Order with anticipation.

Cuttlefish may just be the most interesting animal you never thought about. They are molluscs from the same family as octopus and squid which explains their eight arms and two tentacles with suckers. They are also among the most intelligent invertebrates.

Cuttlefish have a unique internal shell, the cuttlebone, which is porous and is made of aragonite, one of the three forms of calcium carbonate. The fish regulates its buoyancy by changing the gas-to-liquid ratio in the cuttlebone's chambers. You may well remember them among flat shells on the seashore or hanging in the cages of budgerigars, small Australian parrots, for fun and beak strengthening. Incidentally, budgies are the world's third most popular pet.

Another unusual practice is to make casts for metal from the shell. A model is pushed into the cuttlebone and removed to leave an impression. Molten metal can then be poured in to make jewellery or other precious objects.

Cuttlefish use ink to distract predators by forming a cloud behind which they swim away. The ink is farmed for use as flavouring for rice and pasta, giving a black tint and sweet taste. In Greek and Latin, the word for cuttlefish is *sepia*, the pigment produced when the ink is distilled and used by all the Renaissance painter superstars.

whale restaurant, tokyo. © Theron Godbold.

Before you munch into a cuttlefish, reflect that that are often referred to as the chameleons of the sea because of their ability within one second to change their skin colour to match their surroundings. They also make the colour change to communicate with other cuttlefish, especially to give warnings.

My *sushi* bar seemed to have had a recent large delivery of cuttlefish for I was able to try four different dishes: dried and shredded as a starter; roe in *miso* soup; battered and stir fried with butter, chili, red peppers and spring onions; and an unusual *sushi* offering, fried babies on top of the customary *wasabi* and short-grained sticky Japanese rice.

local markets

brill, aylesbury duck, monkfish, red mullet, sild, dover sole, sprat, rainbow trout, whitebait

Not all new species for the table come from some interesting adventure or an out-of-the-way restaurant. Everyday life is more mundane. Half an hour's drive away from my home there's a pick your own farm that hosts a Saturday fish market run by that dying breed, a fishmonger; in this case a fishmongeress.

Her display slab is a far cry from the dismal standard collection at what little remains of the 'fresh' selection at the local supermarkets, gasping for breath alongside the ready-made meals, stuffed with sugar, salt and preservatives. What treats await? Boneless kippers, tired cod fillets, mass Greek-raised seabream, loch-farmed salmon soaked with artificial red colouring, Vietnamese rubber prawns saved from some antibiotic-sated chemical stew, bottom-feeding mackerel with a risk of scombroid poisoning, scraps of cheap-cut white fish tail left over from cat meat, grandly called 'fish soup mix' and, perhaps as a special offer, a small net bag of cultivated mussels, many of the thin shells already broken or beginning to open.

Support your local fishmonger!

Brill is a close relative of the turbot, has a smooth, dark-brown skin with intense white speckling, and as with most other flatfish, its underside is creamy-white. It looks good in a display and is a particular favourite, but a whole fish can set you back even though it can feed four people or more. Buy while you can as wild stocks are limited due to overfishing and inferior farming becomes the norm. The flesh is superior, firm-textured and sweet-tasting.

Monkfish (Lophius, anglerfish, fishing-frogs, frog-fish, sea-devil) must be one of the all-time ugliest fish in its natural state. The squat, unattractive head, usually blackish with a gaping mouth is overhung by a tentacle-like bone extension which dangles, angler like, enticing inquisitive prey within reach of

brill. © Planetseafishing.

an explosive snap. The meat comes from the tail which seems to start immediately behind the head and sits either side of a sturdy gelatinous central bone. This flesh is what the buyer usually sees, easily sliced away and cut into impersonal firm chunks. Its taste is clean rather than fishy. Importantly, it doesn't break down so is popular in curries and spicy stews.

Overfishing is now a problem. Monkfish may soon become yet another expensive rarity. The problem is greedy fisherfolk from far away who use the wrong nets and scoop up more than is necessary. In 2007, the supermarket chain Asda banned the fish from its stores for this reason.

Red mullet is a light-pink fish with a striped fin and a jacket of scales. It has a fine and delicately flavoured, white, textured flesh, some would say delicious, especially when caught and cooked in the northern Mediterranean. The fish is part of the goat fish family and is unrelated to the grey mullet.

A recipe is unnecessary. Like all smaller fish, it should be grilled until the skin crinkles and the flesh can be lifted with a fork. No sauce is needed, the red mullet holds its own. Serve with your favourite green stuff.

The Romans reared them in ponds where they were attended by slaves, caressed by their owners and taught to come to be fed at the sound of a keeper's voice or a bell. They were slow-learning and needed too much attention, claimed Pliny.[46] However, on the table, some thought them worth their weight in silver. The price for a single fish in the time of Caligula was reportedly enormous. Consul Asinius Celer paid eight thousand sesterces.[47]

Sild are fish probably unknown to those who don't buy them in sardine-like tins, the type with the roller key that always breaks on a stubborn lid or a ring pull that cuts your finger. Most usually, sild are immature herrings, often preserved in oil, tomato sauce or pickled. Because of their small size, defining their species can be problematic, so anchovies and mackerel, for instance, may

---

[46] Pliny the Elder, *Natural History*, IX, 64-69.
[47] Suetonius, *Tiberius*, 34.

be mixed in. The Scandinavians love them with their high omega-3, proteins and vitamins. They are a little milder in taste than full-grown sardines.

My favourite cooking method, and my mother's, is to chop them up with an equal amount of raw onion and to grill on thin buttered toast with an abundance of oil and sprinkled with black pepper and curly parsley.

Dover sole, the common sole, is a flatfish with a greyish-brown upper side and its two eyes close together on the right side of its head. It was traditionally most landed in Dover in the English Channel. It is usually caught by bottom trawling and is prized as a food fish, served whole or in easily cut fillets. A small sole is commercially called a 'slip', hence a young girl is a 'slip of a thing'.

The flesh is mild, buttery and sweet and is versatile in the frying pan where it holds together well in cooking. One favourite is *sole meunière*: dredge the fillets (or whole fish) in flour and pan-fry in a brown butter sauce until golden, adding capers which crisp up and bring texture as well as a pleasant acidity.

In 2010, Greenpeace International added the common sole to its seafood red list of those fish that are commonly sold in supermarkets around the world, but which have a high risk of being sourced from unsustainable fisheries.

Sprats are small forage fish that shoal in great numbers with other fish, swimming continuously as they are attacked by gulls and gannets while, from beneath, cod is their top predator. They have a smooth flavour, high in the good oils and fats, and are easily mistaken for baby sardines. Sprats are particularly favoured around the Baltic Sea where they are commonly smoked and preserved in oil which retains a strong smoky flavour. At their best, sprats are fresh, in *rigor mortis*, beheaded and gutted, rolled in flour, and shallow fried, and served with lemon slices as a starter.

Rainbow trout are native to the cold-water tributaries of the Pacific Ocean where they are often known as a steelhead, a fish that returns to fresh water to spawn after a few years in the ocean. As a result, in China, rainbow trout can be sold by law as salmon. Wild-caught and hatchery-reared forms have been transplanted and introduced for food or sport in

aylesbury duck. © Irid Escent.

at least forty-five countries. If released, these true predators are included in the list of the top hundred most globally invasive species, preying on and out-competing natives and transmitting contagious diseases.

Rainbows can be cooked like any other trout. Their flesh is tender with a mild somewhat nutty flavour. Wild, the fish is gamier and stronger and is preferred by many.

The main difference between whitebait and, say, sild or sprats is that they are eaten whole, heads, fins, bones and bowels. The name is a collective term for immature fry below about fifty millimetres. They swim together in large shoals and are easily caught using fine-meshed fishing nets.

monkfish. © Alexander Mayrhofer.

In the UK today, whitebait principally refers to the fry of young sprats, usually herring. Tests in 1903 found boxes of whitebait contained as many as thirty-one species of immature fish: eel, plaice, whiting, herring, sprat and bass along with shrimp, crab, octopus and jellyfish. Londoners planned summer excursions down the Thames to eat them. An annual whitebait festival takes place in Southend.

Whitebait, a favourite of restauranteurs for their simplicity of cooking and cheapness, are normally deep-fried, coated in flour or a light batter, and served very hot with sprinkled lemon juice and bread and butter. They are hard to buy fresh as they are mostly frozen on board immediately after catching.

The authentic Aylesbury duck has white feathers and a pink beak, not bought from the Petersfield fish slab, but from a nearby butcher. Mrs Beaton thought highly of its meat,

> *The duck is deservedly a universal favourite. Its snowy plumage and comfortable comportment make it a credit to the poultry-yard while its broad and deep breast, and its ample back, convey the assurance that your satisfaction will not cease at its death. In parts of Buckinghamshire, this member of the duck family is bred on an extensive scale; not on plains or commons, but in the abodes of cottagers. Round the walls of living rooms,*

and of the bedroom even, are fixed rows of wooden boxes, lined with hay; and it is the business of the wife and children to nurse and comfort the feathered lodgers, to feed the little ducklings, and to take the old ones out for an airing.[48]

red mullet, roman mosaic.

The flesh is pale, soft and tender with little grain and is less fatty than other duck types. The fat is located in a thin layer under the skin. The white feathers were in high demand for quilts. The opening of a railway to Aylesbury in 1839 enabled cheap and quick transport to London markets and, until World War One, duck rearing became highly profitable.

My favourite duck recipe has chopped sage under skin-scored duck breast coated with sea salt surrounded by many black olives, the whole laid on tin foil in a steep dish (to stop splashing) and then filled with strong red wine and cooked for a quarter of an hour in a fan oven at two hundred and twenty degrees.

---

48 Beeton, Isabella, *Mrs Beeton's Book of Household Management* (1861), p. 935.

memories of the med

dormouse, grouper, octopus, sardine, seabass, squid

For many, the Mediterranean says holidays and holidays means sunshine, beaches and parties. I go with the sunshine although warmth away from the burning glare might describe it better. I don't go with beaches, except for diving off or walking along. I certainly don't go with high-octane parties which marks my card. My interest is primarily archaeology and history followed by food. Luckily, the Mediterranean has the best of all three.

Where better to start, then, than with an edible dormouse. It was a back street restaurant, three tables in the street, two occupied by local coffee drinkers, a menu chalked on a stand by the side of multi-coloured beads looking lifeless and a little soiled in the single doorway.

Traffic noise was down to a distant hum. There was not a tourist in sight which was shocking and welcome considering what I had just been through.

Perhaps there is no street as thronged with people as the steady winding climb up the cobbled *Via Dolorosa* in Jerusalem. It represents the supposed route of Jesus on his way to his crucifixion on the site of today's Church of the Holy Sepulchre. The slow journey is a blast of religious commercialism struggling that day in the unrelenting *sharav*, a hot dry desert wind: the din of the barkers, children clutching at pockets and purses, the bloodied bodies of devotees in loin cloths dragging life size crosses between pink and white narrow walls, tawdry artefacts spilling towards passers-by like streams of lava, the synagogues, followed by the churches and the small mosques as each station of remembrance is passed. In this constant scrap between money and the three faiths, God and the prophet are surely the losers.

The cool inside the restaurant was a blessed relief after the mayhem of the mount. Had I really ordered a dormouse or was it a guinea pig or a hamster?

edible dormouse. © Bouke ten Cate.

Dormice were a favourite delicacy of the Romans, kept in special *gilaria*, and eaten in the autumn when they were at their fattest and tastiest. The meat was also thought to be an aphrodisiac. Dormice are easily found today on menus in Slovakia and Croatia. In England, the animal is prolific near Tring in Hertfordshire since they escaped from the private collection of British banker Lionel Rothschild in 1902 with ten thousand of the critters suspected between Beaconsfield and Luton.

A case could be made for either hamster or guinea pig in Israel.

Zoologist Israel Aharoni collected a litter of Syrian hamsters while on expedition. He used them as laboratory animals in Jerusalem, but some escaped through a hole in the floor. The majority of all domestic golden hamsters are thought to have descended from this one batch.

There is a good story that the discovery of the Dead Sea Scrolls over seventy years ago comes down to a guinea pig hunt. The fifteen thousands scrolls, some whole, some in fragments, are a set of ancient Jewish manuscripts, some later included in the Bible, discovered in twelve caves at Qumran in the desert near the sea on the West Bank. They were found in jars by chance by Bedouin shepherds who were searching for wild guinea pigs.

Roasted or fried guinea pigs, *cuy*, are common in South America today and for the last six thousand years, chopped in five, four legs and a head, served with potatoes and corn. Capybaras and squirrels are also on the menu.

My delicious dormice, I had two as a starter, came Roman style, poached with a variety of herbs, spices and sesame oil and a smattering of honey.[49] A friend claimed, in 2001, to have eaten skewered dormouse at The Connaught Hotel in London.

---

49 Apicius, Coelius, *Cooking and Dining in Imperial Rome* (Guttenberg 2009), Chapter IX, 'Stuffed dormouse', p. 396.

By contrast, a little over two thousand kilometres to the west in Tunis I had my first wild seabass. It was the year of the Arab Spring and the streets were still lined with barricades and twitchy soldiery. Streaks of blood on paving stones waited patiently for a heavy rain to wash them clean.

Seabass is a common enough fish when farmed in crowded colonies off the Greek coast, but it is a different and altogether better tasting animal when caught that morning by line.[50] The outdoor restaurant was chosen by the local guide, a supposed doctor of archaeology (he came with a higher fee), who insisted on trying the local *loup de mer*, 'sea wolf' or 'seabass'. Even after just a few days, our relationship was already a little tense.

The first day in Tunis was spent at the Bardo National Museum, the second museum of the African continent after the Egyptian Museum in Cairo.[51] The Bardo houses one of the largest collections of Roman mosaics in the world thanks to excavations at sites in Carthage, Hadrumetum, Dougga and Utica. Many people have a particular obsession, mine is mosaics with three shelves of books on the subject at home. The guide was arrogant, bored and, often, plain wrong. We had words which at one stage involved calling in a curator as an arbitrator.

Five years later, the Bardo was also the site of a Tunisian terrorist attack when twenty-two people, mostly European tourists, were executed. Two of the three terrorists also died, but one escaped. The murder was personal to me as it took place soon after the *Charlie Hebdo* magazine raid in Paris when many journalists were killed.[52]

The second day, the guide explored the ruins of *Carthage*, one of the most important trading hubs of the ancient Mediterranean and one of the most affluent cities of the classical world. The port was fascinating, but had to be reimagined after being first destroyed in a siege by the Roman Republic in 46 BC. The National Museum in the town saw another disagreement, in truth a full-

grouper. © Jarek Tuszyński.

---

50 See chapter 'island love affairs'.
51 See chapter 'out of africa'.
52 Heal, Chris, *Reappearing* (C&S 2020), pp. 152-57.

scale row, as the guide spouted at length descriptions which were at odds with the captions beneath exhibits.

With trips planned to the oval amphitheatre of *El Jem*, one of the best Roman stone ruins in the world, and then to *Dougga*, the best-preserved Roman small town in Africa, I anticipated a final showdown.

The seabass was served whole and freshly fried with plentiful baked lemon in a stone-seated blue and white courtyard. Interestingly, we were offered chopsticks. After the flesh had been picked clean, the guide was obviously distressed. I asked him what was the matter.

'You haven't eaten the skin or the head,' he said. 'It's the best part.'

I offered the remains to him and he fell like a wolf on the plate, sucking each bone naked and crunching several. He clearly thought I was mad and he well may have been right.

The next day, it all fell apart. After a spell of lunatic driving, he screamed to a halt at the roadside with his head in his hands on the steering wheel. After questioning, I realised he was diabetic, I am one myself, hadn't been taking his medication and was in a serious way. I had to force feed him some of my own chocolate bars. That lunchtime, I found him in the restaurant toilet snorting cocaine.

I thought of the guide a couple of years later when I was in Rome viewing mosaics in some of the more obscure churches. Two learned tourists, professors no doubt, where having a full-on row with a tour tout who wouldn't give ground. I left them to it and went for lunch.

The plate of whole squid, stuffed with a cous cous, nut and soft fruit concoction, under a delicate black ink sauce, was lip-smacking. I have tried several times to recreate it, but without success. As a final goodbye, I had an almost too sweet crème brûlée.

The squid set me reminiscing of a time when hitchhiking was the safe and inexpensive way of travel. I was in Thessaloniki on my way to Istanbul. The trip almost ended in disaster. I had taken a space on the roof of a hotel, known to the travelling crowd as 'The Tent'. It was very cheap. Drugs were plentiful. LSD was in its hey day and little understood.[53] A young German who had a sleeping

---

53 Lysergic acid diethylamide is commonly known as LSD and by the slang names 'acid' and 'lucy'. It is a manufactured hallucinogenic compound derived from ergot, known for its powerful psychological effects. It was historically significant in psychiatry and 1960's counterculture. Remember the Beatle's song, *Lucy in the Sky with Diamonds*?

common octopus. © Albert Kok.

bag next to me decided that he could fly and I watched as he failed through three storeys. The Turkish authorities took a dim view and threw the tenants over the border into Bulgaria or Greece. We were all back for a reunion party within two weeks.

At Thessaloniki, short of money, I resorted to selling too much blood in a local hospital which left me weak in body and mind. I found overnight accommodation on the floor of a large shower at the back of a restaurant. The main dish was octopus, stewed in a red pot on an open fire. The trick I later found was slow cooking, anything too rapid causes the tentacles to toughen and become very chewy. It's a dish that takes a strong sauce and any variety of vegetables that are lying around the kitchen.

In some cultures, octopus is eaten live. One has to be careful as some of the tentacle suckers are extremely powerful in a death spasm. People have choked to death as suction cups attached to the throat and blocked their airway.

The Mediterranean is really about fish, salads, oil, summer fruits and wine. I have an endless debate with myself about which fish is the best tasting when simply grilled. I think I plump for butterfish, eaten to perfection in Walvis Bay in southern Africa, but a close second is the grouper which I have rarely eaten because it is seldom found on European menus.[54] The last time was in Bodrum, back in Turkey, but during a more monied visit.

Bodrum was a delightful ancient town before the skyscraper hotels made it their home. It was founded by the Greeks and was once home to the 'Mausoleum at Halicarnassus', also known as the 'Tomb of Mausolus', one of the Seven Wonders of the Ancient World. It is, like Dubrovnik, a complete tourist hell hole in summer as the jets and cruise liners call.

I had joined a small party that had gradually worked its way down Turkey's Aegean coast calling at some of the major archaeological sites: Çanakkale, Troy, Assos, Pergamon, Ephesus, Sardis, Nysa, Prien, Miletus, Euromos and finishing at Bodrum Kalesi, the crusader castle of St Peter.

The hotel near Bodrum was a seething buffet and a fight for smeared seats at just emptied tables. I caught a taxi into town, more in hope than expectation. But, I was wrong. Through a quiet courtyard, was a small, sea-view affair. The catch was carefully displayed and, in the middle, a metre of stout-bodied grouper. These are hunters and, reportedly, the largest will attack humans. Their big mouths pull their prey in from a distance. The taste was excellent and firm with crisped skin and without sauce.

grilled sardines. © Real Greek recipes.

Grouper, like barracuda, moray eel, seabass and sturgeon can also harbour ciguatera from ciguatoxins which have no taste or smell, and cannot be destroyed by conventional cooking. There is no specific treatment for ciguatera fish poisoning. The symptoms, all the usual horrible things, can last from weeks to years, and in extreme cases as long as twenty years, often leading to long-term disability. Most people do recover slowly over time.

Butterfish and grouper (and *fruits de mer*) may be top of the taste tree, but there is another measure which can mean almost as much: situation and company. On those terms, the humble fresh sardine grilled with

---

54 Chapter 'lucky restaurants'.

lemon and oregano on the beach is hard to beat. If the meal is taken with your own extended family on a relaxed holiday with no sulks in sight and plenty of cold beer on tap, it might just be heaven. It could be a time of forgiveness.

The meal was at Albufeira on the Portuguese Algarve coast. It was Christmas week and the sun was shining, not hot, but no wind, the sort of day when one understands why so many have packed bags and mortgages and moved home forever.

Sardines are one of the healthiest fish, packed with omega-3 fatty acids to counteract heart problems. Soak the whole fresh fish in plenty of cold water first which helps to thicken the skin. Dry off. Sardine skin is delicate so remove the scales with circular movements of a thumb rather than a knife. Scatter with sea salt. Leave the head on and use it to grab the ungutted fish to turn it. Fish placed side by side on a hot grill need only five minutes, half of that on each side or, to keep down the flaming oil if basting, cook at a lower temperature for around twelve minutes. Olive oil is best for preventing sticking. Drizzle the result with a lemon and olive oil sauce. Serve with flatbread and a confident salad.

Eat with your fingers, admire the view, slurp beer and talk to your family.

niger nibbles

crocodile, rock python

Kabu and Tabu, early teenage boys known collectively as the 'BuBu', perched high on the bow and called instructions against obstructions near the surface to the men armed with poles. The Niger River was relatively clear; its rocky headwaters carried only a tenth as much sediment as the Nile.

In one of the calm stretches, we came against a sleeping crocodile and BuBu asked me if I would like some fresh meat. It was a remarkable demonstration of skill as we floated alongside the inert creature. BuBu waited their moment and both stepped on the horny back and rammed their spears simultaneously into the crocodile's eyes. Nimbly, they stepped back into the pinasse as the animal twitched, rolled over, and was dead.

With considerable yelling and delight, the boat pulled the carcass to shore and the boys and a Bozo crew member directed the skinning. It was a mighty roasted feast, yes, tasting like chicken, but pleasantly fishy with olives, the whole saddened by the bones of a small, decayed human hand in the stomach.

I also ate crocodile at a commercial farm at Can Tho in Vietnam. As a tourist, I watched from a fence down into a pit as hundreds of the beasts lay in the sun or crawled over each other. In the café, it was like chicken again, but tougher and not worth the money. The day after I left, a keeper cleaning the fence, slipped and fell.

The next day, BuBu shouted again from the bow in excitement. This was a rare sight even for these experienced river boys. Two West African manatee, fifteen feet, each weighing nearly 800 pounds, popped up for a look.

'That is unusual,' mused our captain. 'They are on the extinction list. They usually prefer salt water, but being herbivores they sometimes come up above the oil pollution and get trapped closer to the Kainji dam.'

west african crocodile. © Marco Schmidt.

Below the dam, the Niger is easily navigable all the year round and runs through a monotonous broad and shallow valley between five and ten miles wide. It was late and we stopped at a river police station near the bend at Jessao, an unseen town. The men went ashore to the small barracks while we and the captain slept on the boat. I was sitting on my bunk, beginning to undress, having finally got BuBu to sleep, when there was a fearful scream from the shore. I sensed it was a snake for I had been dreaming about vipers and adders and past horrors.

Bathed in the light from above the barrack door, this was no viper, but almost four metres of African rock python entwined around a slumped member of our crew. Blood wept from every facial cavity of the squeezed body. With every gasp, the snake tightened its grip.

'He went for a pee,' shouted one of the guards. 'We told him not to go off the veranda. We told him there was a python's nest there.'

The man was hysterical. 'He stood right on it.'

The evidence was on the ground, a long scrape in the earth, about thirty elongated eggs, several broken into a khaki mess. The python's skin was covered in thick blotches of olive and chestnut. Its head, dark brown, lined with yellow, shaped like a spear, was beginning to disarticulate as it sized up its meal. It looked like the snake had coiled the man's leg as he stood, urinating and unsuspecting, and kept on climbing.

As I stepped forward, the captain fumbled his pistol out of its holster, but was unsure where to fire. It was a long time since I had got up close and personal. Pythons carry no venom, have no bite, their sharp, inner teeth curve backwards to ease the swallow. I faced the animal, inches away, and gazed into the hypnotic eyes. Within seconds, its grip loosened, steadily relinquishing its prey. Its eyes never left mine and the head swayed to keep contact. As the python moved to the undergrowth, the captain lined up his gun, but I pushed it down softly.

'Bad luck,' I advised.

'I can see that it could be awkward to get on your wrong side,' he replied. 'You have some surprising skills. In Hausa, they call it *bòòríí*, 'spiritual power'.'

He quoted from the *Qur'an*, 'From the evil of the slinking whisperer who whispers in the breast of mankind of djinn and men.'

As I looked up, I saw BuBu standing open-mouthed on the cutter's deck. The man jerked, moaned and died, I suspected of heart failure.

'Damn. He was not the best policeman, but at least he did what he was told.'

I went back to the boat, then heard a shot. The captain followed me on board.

'It's a question of prestige, of leadership,' he explained.' The men needed revenge for their comrade. I have ordered it skinned and we'll all eat it tomorrow in the man's memory.'

Next day, we chased the river at breakneck speed. About seventy miles from Jebba, with its hydroelectric power station, the Niger is joined by the Kaduna, Hausa for 'crocodile', where we smashed onwards, oblivious. It was little different a few hours later at Lokoja where the Niger forms a 'Y' with its principal tributary, the Benue, as we cut through an inland salt lake full of islets and shoals.

The cook brought us python steaks.

female northern african rock python.
© www.bigsnake.ch.

'Do you know,' I offered, 'if you hadn't told me this was python, I'd have said it was crocodile, both not far off chicken, but this is more fatty, nothing gamey, and better tasting.' There was nodding all around.

The river began its descent from a two thousand-foot high plateau, due south to the sea three-hundred and forty miles away. We tore, crew laughing, through a restricted valley, enclosed by hills. The landscape flattened at Onitsha, the largest town on the Niger's banks in Nigeria and the third largest overall after Bamako and Niamey. We emerged from sandstone cliffs into rainforest at Aboh where the delta began and its hundreds of capillaries leaked river water into the Gulf of Guinea.

paddy bounty

rice-field rat

Vang Vieng might be the world's most beautiful village, much quieted by government edict since its hippie party days and gradually cleared of ordnance since Laos became the most ruined country on the planet. From 1964 to 1973, American bombers dropped over two million tons of cluster bombs, more than all the bombs dropped in World War Two.

These munitions fell in a case which was designed to open in mid-air releasing thousands of bomblets packed with nuts, nails and bolts. The bombs detonated with a spring which needed to spin several times before exploding. Some cases malfunctioned and hit the ground in one piece. Children mistook them for toys, played with them and made the final turn.

In a covert 'quiet' war, the Central Intelligence Agency, the civilian foreign intelligence service of the USA, attempted to wrest control from the communist Pathet Lao. The Americans lost, as they lost Vietnam and Cambodia. The Pathet Lao, officially the Lao People's Liberation Army, assumed political power in 1975.

Towering karst mountains rise around seas of rippling paddies. Karst is a land of limestone, a soft rock that erodes as the rainwater seeps in. Above ground, there are steep, rocky cliffs and, beneath, caves, streams and sinkholes.

Conical hats bob above the crops. Stilted huts sprout along the banks of the determined Nam Song. Women set traps for freshwater prawns and sometimes fish for *khai phun*, moss from the irrigation streams and throw it on hot stones to dry.[55] The older children walk slowly home from school, one arm weighted with books, the other pulling the family buffalo from where it had grazed

---

55 Tom Vater, *The Man with the Golden Mind* (Osprey Group 2014).

while they studied. Younger siblings catch lizards and rice-rats to carry to the leisurely evening market.

I sat in that calm half-hour before twilight with a pre-dinner gin. The veranda breeze was just brisk enough to keep the mosquitoes at bay. I soaked in the view of fishing canoes and children splashing at the water's edge. A slight rainbow, a *caihong*, remembered a late afternoon shower.

Amongst the canoes, young Western backpackers floated on inner tubes, beers and joints in hand. Someone drowned almost every week, overcome for choice between cheap opium, hallucinogenic mushrooms, marijuana and alcohol. Occasionally, rich, haggard parents visited Vang Vieng from Germany or Sweden to take the body of their loved child home.

rice-field rat.

I heard the clump on the wooden veranda of a metal foot which I saw was hidden beneath a brightly flowered, full-length skirt. PajYeeb's black hair was curled over her left shoulder and tied with a red ribbon, a subtle announcement that she was unmarried. Her face showed the beginning of skin lines at the corners of her black eyes and her top lip. These wrinkles were the signs of long-term suffering, but she had not forgotten how to smile.

PajYeeb was a Hmong, a long distant descendant of the Chinese incomers from around the Vietnamese border, a tribal survivor of the great and lost fight against the Pathet Lao. It was her bare right arm which caught the eye. I tried hard not to look, but the evidence was plain to see. As well as having lost a leg to a cluster bomb, PajYeeb was a badly burned survivor of the yellow rain.

With the end of the war, the Vietnamese and Pathet Lao forces announced plans to wipe out the Hmong in revenge for them siding with the Yankees. The next year, they started dropping coarse mists of oily yellow rain on Hmong villages to force the clans from their mountain hideouts. The rain contained trichothecene mycotoxins, bleeding agents, defoliants and skin burners.

'*Txais tos*. I am most pleased to meet you,' I said. 'But, tell me, doesn't *yeeb* mean opium. For me, it is an unusual name.'

'PajYeeb is a little difficult to translate and can mean many things, often emotions,' she explained. '*Paj* means clear like the blue sky without clouds but, together with *yeeb*, we use it most often to mean opium blossom. The flower is beautiful, but also contains strength or, some would say, danger.'

She lowered her head briefly and smiled at her self-deprecating humour.

'Opium is an important crop for the Hmong people. It takes away the pain.'

We sipped our drinks slowly and sought some slight solace in the bustling river, the black karst, the blue, gradually darkening sky, noticing everything except each other. A restaurant boy called from the street.

'You will stay and have dinner? I would be honoured if you would be my guest.'

PajYeeb accepted with a broad smile. I gave the boy a small fold of Lao kips, LAKs, and held up one finger from each hand to signify the number and sex of the diners. The lady who ran the restaurant without tables would decide the variety and extent of the meal and the boy would run the errand. There were over twenty-thousand kips to the US dollar and, even then, each kip was sub-divided into one hundred atts. Food was cheap, especially for visitors with faraway bank accounts.

Tonight's choice centred on plump field rats, strong on salt and chili, with rice and river greenery. The barbequed meat, gutted and without head and legs, was golden-brown, clean because of the animal's diet, fatty near the skin, sweet and delicious. The alternative, also a favourite, is to sauté the meat for thirty minutes with seeds, lemongrass and garlic, and then fry or bake.

Sated, a contented silence fell.

Rice-rats are everywhere in the paddy fields, a true pest. Their top fur is yellow-brown and black. Large groups scavenge at night for termites, insects, nuts and rice. Up to ten young can arrive every few weeks. They are most easily caught in seine nets and cage traps at harvest when they swarm.

The boy returned briefly with a much-used plastic bag to collect the paper plates, tinfoil containers, chopsticks and mouth and hand wipes. A small tip completed the unspoken transaction.

in praise of pig

boar, pig, warthog

Pig might be the national animal of the British Midlands. At one time, it seemed that every back yard, no matter how small, had space for one or two porkers, enough to keep the family through the winter. The most popular was the red-coloured Tamworth.

I spent some of my teenage years in the 1960s in West Bromwich. In the posher end of town where my family lived there was no sight of a domestic pig. However, I made my pocket money (and a bit more) running a window cleaning business. This was the Black Country after all. The steady smoke from the thousands of chimneys kept me in employment. I worked weekends, and evenings in the summer, with my ladder, bucket and shammy leather in long terraces of small workers' homes around the factories and canals in Oldbury, Tipton and Smethwick.

The story here was very different from my home. I frequently had to park my ladder in a stye so as to reach the upper windows. It was completely natural therefore that the region's favourite bar snack was pork scratchings. These were not the anaemic chemical offerings in little plastic bags of today's pubs. These were the real thing, often sold loose on the counter, great chunks of burnt skin with generous meat attached where the bodies had been scrapped after scalding and still with plenty of bristles in sight.

There was a low-key market which ran down from Dartmouth Square towards, I think, the bus stops, where scratchings were sold off a large inclined wooden slab, open to the air. Small shovels were on hand for you to fill your paper bag.

At home, I can't remember bacon being on the breakfast or dinner menu, but then my mother's cooking skills were always suspect. It was a great day for her when she discovered the tin opener. She was reputed to be able to burn water, so what chance for a rasher?

While I was waiting to go to pilot training at Hamble on the Solent, I got a job as a delivery driver with a West Bromwich metal casting company. I had several minor accidents. In later life, I felt sorry for the management. They must have been shocked that a future commercial flyer should have so many bumps and scrapes in their lorry. One of my jobs as a junior employee was to drive on a Saturday morning to a local sandwich shop, armed with the factory's lunch requirement. To assemble the volume of orders and get them back while still warm was a task beyond me. However, I do remember the revelation of the bacon and tomato baps with *Lea and Perrins* sauce. Life was never the same again.

It is a close run thing, but I nominate a breakfast I had at a hotel in Gullane in East Lothian as the bacon champion. Four rashers beautifully cooked on a warm plate, crisp white linen table cloth and napkin, two perfect runny fried eggs, fried toast, black and white pudding slices, mushrooms, a substantial pork sausage (of course), tomatoes and baked beans. I left the beans. I needed room for the toast and marmalade. I can still smell the coffee.

Another piggy favourite which has gone by the way was boiled hock, then as cheap as chips. The process I was taught by a senior journalist at my first newspaper was to place two hocks in a saucepan of very lightly bubbling water. Then go to the pub for an hour or two. Back at home, the hock meat fell from the bone into a ready covering of buttered bread and English mustard alongside a carry out of draught beer.

The surprise to me is that I am not that fond of pork meat, roasted or as a chop. There is something about the smell. I think it must be close to the imagined aroma of burnt human flesh; not, of course, that I have ever experienced that. Except, if the fat on the chop has been crisped properly, I could eat that alone. And, then, there's pork meat chunks that have been marinated for a day before cooking in a vindaloo sauce.

About one and a half billion pigs are slaughtered each year, about a third of them in China. It seems a shame as the average pig is more intelligent than a pet dog. Pigs distinguish each other as individuals, spend time in play and like to live in small communities. They have good long-term memory and can identify locations of objects and can solve mazes. They even recognise themselves in a mirror. Did you know that Swindon is in the *Domesday Book* as *Suindune*, derived from the Old English *swine* and *dun*, 'pig hill'?

Of great importance to truffle fanatics, pigs can be trained to sniff out these underground delights and then not to eat them. This is a double edged sword for the pig because truffles and pork are often the main ingredients in charcuterie products like terrines, galantines, pâtés and confits. The supreme Italian pork salamis are fermented and air-dried to be eaten raw. The original varieties include *Genovese, Milanese* and *Cacciatorino* with spicier kinds from the south such as *Calabrese, Napoletano* and *Peperone*. It is a great delight in, say, Verona to start a long dinner with a plate of cold meats.

I can offer two other top culinary common pig experiences.

In Johannesburg, I had a trencherman friend who introduced me to many of the city's better restaurants. Perhaps his favourite was the members-only 'Rand Club', very colonial when we went there. It was founded only a year after the city was declared in 1902. The current building, the third iteration due to its popularity and exclusiveness, stands on a corner of Loveday Street. It is in an Edwardian neo-baroque style inspired by Michaelangelo's Church of the Sacred Heart in Florence and by the Reform Club in London. It's where the Queen used to stay when in town.

The ground-floor restaurant is all that you would expect, wood panelled, slightly hushed, with members getting a twenty per cent discount. We almost always had the same meal: a large ham brought to the table and thin carved with just the best mayonnaise. There might have been some small potatoes on the plate.

Back in the late 1960s, very hungry and short of money, I took an overnight ferry from Igoumenitsa in Greece to Bari. The theory was the money spent on the ferry would save the extra cash needed to travel and stay on a trip around the armpit of Italy. At Bari, I stuck out

wild boar. © Valentin Panzirsch.

common warthog. © Sharp Photography.

my thumb and waited for a lift for the two hundred and fifty kilometres over the spine of Italy to Naples. After a few hours my luck was in. I slept as best I could in the cab of the lorry. An hour short of Naples, my driver pulled in to a scruffy roadside café outside of the town of Avellino. It was a flat plain with distant mountains. I slumped at an outside table wondering how much some food might cost.

The driver returned, handed me a beer and a large sandwich of flat bread filled with shredded pork from a barbeque. He patted me on the head and told me to enjoy. The hot fat was so rich it ran out of the sandwich and down my fingers. I have never, ever, eaten anything so welcome and so delicious.

There's archaeological evidence that pigs were domesticated from wild boar in the Tigris Basin, a serious trouble spot between Iraq and Iran at about the same time as my Italian trip. Over half a million people died in that First Gulf War.

I was on an autumn training course with an American multinational in Belgium. Frankly, I was bored to death. At the bar on the early evening before the last day someone told me about a hotel in a place called Durbuy in the Ardennes. It was named after the local wild boar, the *Hotel Sanglier*. I made a call and got there in time for last orders in the restaurant. Nowhere is very far away in Belgium. The hotel was rustic, full of old beams, not in top decoration, but very acceptable with excellent service.

That first night, I had a thick red *sanglier* stew, slow cooked for many hours, in fact a *ragu* or *civet*, with all the expected ingredients except, perhaps, the addition of bacon lardons, juniper berries and orange peel. I chose a bottle of Savoie *Jongieux Gamay*. The boar flesh had less fat than pork, but was similar in taste if decidedly nuttier. Delicious.

The next day I joined a mushroom hunt in the forest. A selection of a dozen types found formed our starter for that evening. I was told a secret. The dinner was from the same cooking as the day before, left to cool overnight and reheated.

'It's always better the next day.'

It was.

I looked up the hotel on the internet as I wrote this section. All has changed. It's been rebuilt, but is still called the *Hotel Sanglier*. I couldn't see boar on the menu, perhaps out of season. It's now a five-star wellness centre. Ahh well!

I ate a common warthog filet steak in a bush camp at Tswalu in South Africa's Northern Cape. The animal's numbers have risen dramatically and the beasts were causing a nuisance around the five-star tents. The porkiness was there, but also a hint of beef with less fat and not at all gamey. It certainly would win over pork meat for me. I brought the warthog's skull home, picked clean and complete with tusks.

It still rests on the lower shelf of a cabinet. To be so ugly and to be so delicious!

lucky restaurants

butterfish, dog, goose, salmon, sewin, snipe, swan, brown trout, yellowfin tuna

Restaurants: sometimes costly, fashionable, perhaps a place to see or be seen with more than the promise of top class food – *The Ivy* in London is here; others sometimes just a hole-in-the-wall, chosen by instinct or hunger, a step into the unknown for purse and tummy – an eating house in Huế in Vietnam that casually serves dog exemplifies that category. This chapter offers a small selection of those interesting, impromptu choices where I recall adding another unexpected species to my list.

I stepped ashore in Walvis Bay, 'whale bay', in Namibia from a small cruise ship. I know, I know, but I have learned my hard lesson about the joys of cruising. The bay is a haven for sea vessels, protected by a sand spit, making the country's only natural deep-water harbour. Any water free from container ships and their towering Chinese-built terminal was taken by large fishing boats and schools of baleen whales. The city hadn't changed much in twenty years, bigger yes, but still a mass of cranes, rusting freighters and soulless warehouses supporting the scar of the TransNamib railway to Windhoek, the capital.

The area was already known to me from a history I had written on World War One when this part of the world was a captured German colony.[56] Here, the native Herero and Nama tribes were slaughtered for their land. It became the proving ground of Nazi eugenics and concentration camps. In 2021, modern Germany finally agreed to a €1.1 billion 'gesture of reconciliation' for the genocide.

The cheerleader aboard my ship described the town as an important centre of tourism. To be fair, there is an artificial Bird Island, the centre of a guano

---

56 Heal, Chris, *The War of the Raven* (C&S 2023), pp. 22-27.

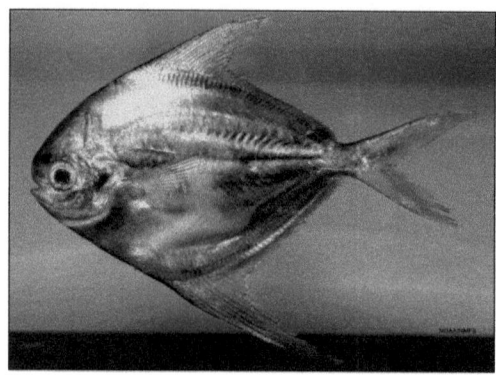
butterfish. © NOAA Photo Library.

collection industry; a salt works under the *Cerebos* brand; and an important and ever-growing export processing zone.

Within half an hour of landing, one of our party was badly mugged in broad daylight in the main street. To escape, I tried to catch a taxi to two of the out-of-town attractions, but the first driver, eyes bloodshot and staring into the middle distance, could only mumble through the cocaine snorted from the packet lying on the front passenger seat.

The first draw, 'Dune 7' (because it's a seven mile drive) is one of the world's highest sand hills, just short of four hundred metres. It's hell to climb. I gave in about a third of the way up its ridge and slid back down. The view of sea and desert from the top is reported amazing.

Not far from the dune's bottom are several old lettuces, two-thousand-year-old lettuces. *Welwitschia mirabilis* can survive for hundreds of years in the arid desert by absorbing water from sea fog and deep groundwater. It grows around one metre tall and has two large leaves, a stem base and a taproot. As the two wide, pale green, fleshy leaves grow, they split over time into multiple segments, making the plant appear to have many more leaves. The ends of these leaves are often dry and dead-looking.

As this is a book about food, I have included a picture which is a lot more lively than the dishevelled specimen I encountered. I didn't eat any. You have to imagine a group of middle-aged, over-heated cruise tourists standing in a circle around a double millennium lettuce, dune in the background, singing 'Happy Birthday'.

Back in town, I split from the group and wandered some dingy backstreets in, paradoxically, super bright sunlight. The restaurant was more of a lean-to only owning up to its occupation by a sheet tacked to a wooden post. It announced, 'Prawns, fried. Butterfish, pan fried'.

Inside all was pristine and deep green and white gingham cloth. The cutlery sparkled. The beer was from down the road, cold, frosted glass, and just right. The prawns were local, brought in that morning, and reminded me of how things used to be before the big Vietnamese farms. Butterfish, also known as sablefish (and, to be clear, *Stromateidae*, as there are many imposters), is a deep-sea fish with one population concentration off west Africa. It is delicate and distinctive; the rich, buttery, oily taste is both sweet and savoury. The fish's high fat content also gives it a smooth, creamy texture that melts in the mouth, making it an absolute hit with this seafood lover. Think wagyu beef mixed with fresh grated black truffles: luxurious and decadent.[57] Meal of the year.

Which is, in truth, more than can be said for the shack I visited in Huế. It was too dark to see if it was clean. I had been looking for somewhere to eat that was frequented by the Vietnamese, but the town was heaving with tourists, mostly American, so perhaps the locals ate at home – except, I hoped, at this spot.

Huế is a good place to visit: the Perfume River, a large complex of imperial palaces, pagodas, tombs and temples. Alongside the moat and thick stone walls is the imperial city with shrines, the Forbidden Purple City and more monuments than is decent. The reason for most of the American tourists is found in modern history. The Battle of Huế in 1968 was a major part of the Tết Offensive launched by North Vietnam and the Việt Cộng. Initially losing control of most of Huế and its surroundings, the combined forces of South Vietnam and the United States gradually recaptured the city after a little over one month of bloody fighting. The near defeat marked the beginning of the decline of the broad early support for the war among the American public.

As a starter, I chose *bánh bèo* made from a combination of rice and tapioca flour and stuffed with marinated shrimps and crispy pork skin cooked in scallion oil and served with a dipping sauce. It's a favourite street food.

Then I came to a dead halt. There are plenty of problematic foods in this book from penguin, through tarantula, to elephant. But dog?

If you see any *Fido* as a loyal companion and beloved family member then your pseudo-ethics may already be up in arms. Your arguments may suggest that humans have a special bond with dogs and that eating them is somehow morally wrong. There are also concerns about animal welfare and the methods of slaughter although this is really a side issue to be applied to any animal reared for food. In this case, I didn't know whether *Fido* was a huggable Spaniel or a street hound born to die.

---

57 Chapter 'sushi paradise'.

I reasoned the proclivities of other cultures was not my direct concern. I had a one-time opportunity. What was the difference in the food chain of dog, horse, cow or the cute prawns I had just polished off with relish and curry sauce. The dog didn't taste like chicken, but was similar to a chewy pork and beef combination with a slightly stronger aftertaste. Some liken the meat to venison, but the chef told me that flavour varied depending on the breed of dog, its diet and the method of preparation. This one was a 'local dog'.

Another problematic food, I understand, is goose, not the cooked bird but those that appear as *foie gras*, 'fat liver', a delicacy much banned around the world, but protected under French law. The problem is that the liver must be fattened by *gavage*, 'force feeding'. A funnel fitted with a long metal or plastic tube is pushed into the bird's oesophagus. Nowadays, using a pneumatic pump, the operation takes two to three seconds. The feed is usually corn boiled with fat to facilitate ingestion; large amounts of fat are deposited in the liver. For the goose, this feeding lasts for up to eighteen days, three times daily. The result is a liver enlarged by a gross ten times. Sadly for the bird, it tastes sublime: rich, buttery and delicate.

Gavage-based *foie gras* raises much more ire than the final killing of the animals. Antagonists disparage the force-feeding, but also suggest intensive housing and slapdash husbandry. The Swiss have banned production since 1978, and specifically force-feeding from 2008. It is legal in only five of the EU member states. Other banning laws exist in Israel, Turkey, Australia and California. In 2022, the Buckingham Palace household confirmed that *foie gras* was not bought by or served in royal residences. A UK poll showed sixty-three per cent of residents favoured a complete ban on its sale.

I first tasted the real thing at a goose farm in Normandy in France, visited unknowingly as a country B&B. It was a rough and ready establishment, but with excellent service and a set meal: *foie gras* as an extensive starter, goose breast with potatoes and large marrowfat peas roasted in goose fat and, for desert, classic French apple *tatin*.

welwitschia mirabilis. © H2GRO.

My only complaint was that the stay cost €200, but the credit card receipt when it came showed two thousand. It took six months to get the extra money back.

I have chosen a 'proper' restaurant for my second *foie gras*, the Gundel near Budapest's main park, which hosted Queen Elizabeth during a royal visit in 1993. The *pâté de foie gras* with warmed squares of thin toast brought real tears of joy. I did reduce the waiter to stunned silence, so much so that he dashed for the *maître d'hôtel*, when I insisted on a large glass of chilled vodka to accompany it. He deigned to try the combination, then a large smile split his face before he rushed to tell the chef of his discovery.

The late Queen's son, Charles, was responsible for my first taste of Scottish wild salmon, served with *sauce verte*. I had lunch with him, and a hundred others, at a premier hotel in Edinburgh during an event I organised. Once enjoyed wild, the farmed variety never again hits the spot in the same way.[58]

Swan meat was regarded as a luxury food in England during the reign of the first Elizabeth. Today, it is covered in half myths, royal pretensions and unavailability. Basically, it's a rich man's game.[59] The swan probably typifies the core 'ethical' argument behind dogs and penguins. The bird is so elegant, so regal, so tranquil, that it transcends the fate of being seen as mere food. The arguments are always conflated. What is the essential difference between eating a goose and a swan?

Many years ago, I was closely involved with a London livery company, one of the ancient craft brotherhoods that has rights in the city and also a large and sumptuous oak-panelled guildhall for very private meetings, hung with dusty portraits and lists of long-forgotten leaders. Word spread by mouth that this year's special banquet would centre on swan prepared in the old Elizabethan way,

> *To bake a Swan Scald it and take out the bones, and parboil it, then season it very well with Pepper, Salt and Ginger, then lard it, and put it in a deep Coffin of Rye Paste with store of Butter, close it and bake it very well, and when it is baked, fill up the Vent-hole with melted Butter, and so keep it; serve it in as you do the Beef-Pie.*[60]

---

58 Heal, Chris, chapter 'Prince Charles and Nigel Corbally Stourton', *Glimpses of the Famous* (C&S 2025), pp. 209-213.
59 Cleaver, Emily, 'The Fascinating, Regal History Behind Britain's Swans', *Smithsonian*, 31/7/2017.
60 Woolley, Hannah, 'The Queen-like Closet or Rich Cabinet Scored with all manner of Rare Receipts for Preserving, Candying and Cookery' (London 1672).

In Britain, it is illegal to intentionally kill or injure a wild swan without a licence.[61] The monarch also has special rights over all wild swans which means that no one can hunt them without permission. The process is mired in bureaucracy. I don't know where the swans came from for our excellent meal, served with studied indifference by white-socked waiters in historic costumes, or what permissions were obtained.

Swan is a lean, low-fat meat, high in protein, rich in copper, iron, zinc, selenium, phosphorous and magnesium with omega-3 fatty acids, vitamin B12 and dietary fibre. It is a healthy option except for the high danger of excessive lead from fishing weights and shotgun pellets. The meat looks like venison, carves like beef and tastes like tuna, or old mutton if you are having a bad day.

In any group of swans, a 'bevy' or a 'wedge', the male, a 'cob', and the female, a 'pen', join for life before mating, perhaps bonding for over twenty years. Some believe that on the death of a partner, a mute swan will sing beautifully – the 'swan song'. This symbol of everlasting love is everywhere in literature: W B Yeats' 'Leda and the Swan' (although more lust than affection); 'Odette', the white swan, and 'Odile', the black, in Tchaikovsky's ballet 'Swan Lake'. In the Finnish epic *Kalevala*, a swan lives in the Tuoni River, the underworld of the dead where whoever kills a swan will also perish.

The pair of lovers have up to seven 'cygnets' each year, the ugly ducklings from the fairy tale, and will viciously attack anything seen as a threat to their chicks. They grow up to a metre and a half, weighing over fifteen kilograms. They are almost entirely herbivorous, eating by up-ending, or dabbling, using their long necks to reach bottom plants although they do eat small aquatic animals that get in the way.

Now, not many people know this. Snipe is one of the most difficult game birds to shoot. It lives in dense vegetation in wet marshes and along rivers and the coast where it is well camouflaged. Alert and easily startled, the bird flies an erratic pattern and rarely stays long in the open. The expert snipe hunter is recognised for his high skills in stealth and markmanship and gives his name to the silent military killer – the sniper.

Snipe are small, migratory wading birds with very long slender bills which allow the tips to stay closed while invertebrates are slurped up. For centuries, snipe was a prized addition to the dinner table, celebrated for its unique and

---

61 Wildlife and Countryside Act 1981.

sewin. © Wolfgang Striewski.

flavourful meat. Due to habitat loss and hunting regulations, it is now much less common.

I found it by surprise on the menu at a gastropub near Aldeburgh in Suffolk and couldn't resist. It was distinctive, rich, earthy, and intensely gamey, like concentrated duck meat with a subtle liver-like quality.

I have mixed feelings about trout. Often the taste is muddy, or at the other end, insipid. I do buy brown trout occasionally from a fishing lake farm shop and enjoy making a pâté in gelatine with chopped vegetables. However, this chapter is about restaurants and I will mention two trout dishes briefly.

For a while I worked at a factory on the Firth of Clyde in Scotland. Whenever, I had business guests and felt it appropriate to eat out for lunch, I would take them to a small old country house at Skelmorlie, just down the coast. Brown trout were kept in two large ponds in the garden which is well enough as the fish is one of the world's worst invasive fishes, like their rainbow cousins.

The fillets were always served cold with new potatoes, parsley and horseradish and perhaps a side salad. Simple but effective. The view from the main window which took in the breadth of the river towards Rothesay and the Isle of Bute was always inspiring. A bottle of Pouilly-Fumé … what more could one want.

Save the planet. Eat brown trout.

In Wales, Fishguard to be precise, sea trout is called 'sewin'. It is a form of brown trout, silvery with faint black spots at sea, but reverting to type with dark and red spots when it returns to freshwater. I had just tied up the inflatable after a hard morning's diving and wanted to try a newly-opened fish restaurant in the High Street in the Old Town. I thought sewin must be some exotic fish, but as it was served whole, it was immediately clear what it was. This one was caught the night before by fly fishing. I had no need to complain. The fish was simply grilled, served with samphire and an aubergine sauce. Outstanding.

common snipe. © Bernard Dupont.

At the beginning of this chapter, I mentioned *The Ivy*. I visited several times when it was in its glorious later period before its temporary closure due to a change in ownership in 1989. It reopened the following year with a transformational design and one hundred seats plus a sixty-seat private dining space upstairs. Mobile phones and cameras were forbidden and there was a smart casual dress code. The modern *Ivy* has since expanded across the United Kingdom and Ireland with its new restaurants known as the *Ivy Collection*. The London restaurant with its excellent food is, naturally, because of its location, popular with theatregoers. It became an institution with *habitués* like Laurence Olivier, Vivian Leigh, Marlene Dietrich, John Gielgud, Lilian Braithwaite, Terence Rattigan, Binkie Beaumont and Noël Coward.

It was here that I met the actor Sir Stephen Fry. I tell the story of our encounter in the toilets elsewhere.[62]

It was a long-held ambition fulfilled when I first sat down at a central table. Along the external walls, in the posh seats, a dozen stars were ensconced at their regular spots, too many to mention and none of whom I met (and pretended not to stare as I tried to remember their names).

This was the first time I had yellowfin tuna, not the blue riband bigeye or bluefin varieties, mentioned elsewhere, but superbly cooked, no knife needed, and married with exquisite creamed spinach.[63]

---

62 Heal, Chris, *Glimpses of the Famous* (C&S 2025), pp. 89-90.
63 Chapters 'island love affair' and 'sushi paradise'.

retribution

alligator, bear, bison, roe deer, hippopotamus, lamprey, mackerel, marlin, scorpion, shark, swordfish, tarantula

When an old, convicted and unrepentant carnivore has eaten many more than one hundred and fifty species just as an experiment, it would not be surprising if the animal world decided, driven by a sense of justice or fairness, to enact a punishment, to take retribution. What is sauce for the goose, is it not also sauce for the gander?

A single-minded lamprey, for instance, might see the consumption of a human as suitable, formal punishment for such a wrongdoing; an act that can be carried out, not as retaliation for a personal slight, but with detachment and as a duty. The result, if a result could be later identified, could thus serve as a deterrent and uphold a little order in an avaricious society. If this was not the case, why then, humans might believe they could travel the world eating wildly anything that crossed their path and then spitting it out if the taste was not up to expectation.

Casual mention of the lamprey enables a case in point and leads to much wickedness. The lamprey is a jawless fish that pre-dates dinosaurs, not an eel as often thought. The adult has a toothed, funnel-like sucking mouth.[64] They feed by boring into the flesh of other fish, or in rarer cases marine animals, or in even rarer cases, humans. The bite is often toxic. Lamprey can be over a metre long and is more difficult to slap away than a simple leech.

Don't write these beasts off as foreign things. They have recently been sighted up the River Wear at Chester-le-Street. During the Norman Conquest, lamprey were found in the River Thames at Petersham. Their first known successful assassination came at this time. William the Conqueror's fourth son, Henry

---

64 The only other living jawless fish is thought to be the hagfish, uneaten by the author.

lamprey. © Tilt Hunt.

I of England, died on campaign in Normandy in 1135.[65] At Lyons-la-Forêt to hunt, he ate a 'surfeit of lampreys' against a doctor's orders who was worried by their richness. Henry suffered an attack and was dead within the week. He was a man of 'great vigour and energy' who was never ill.

Queen Elizabeth II was presented with a lamprey pie by the dubious people of Gloucester to mark her coronation in 1953. Clearly, she ate none of it. Gloucester has been plagued by low government investment, floods and poor river defences ever since.

Infiltration by lamprey goes back to Roman times when there was also Henryesque popularity. Vedius Pollo kept a pool of giant lamprey for eating slaves who had displeased him. Lucius Licinius Crassus was mocked in 54 BC by Gnaeus Domitius Ahenobarbus for weeping over the death of his pet lamprey,

> *So, when Domitius said to Crassus the orator, 'Did you not weep for the death of the lamprey you kept in your fish pond?' Did not you, said Crassus to him again, bury three wives without ever shedding a tear?*[66]

God's hand can be found, at least in Henry's death, as the sea lamprey does not taste at all of fish but of slow-cooked beefsteak in a stew. Meat was expensive, although not for Henry. Lamprey could be eaten during Lent when meat was banned by the Roman church.

Each March, three thousand gourmets, of which I was once one, flood the small village of Montemor-o-Velho in Portugal for a lamprey and rice festival.

---

65 *The Winchester Tales*, p. 185. Hollister, C Warren, *Henry I* (Yale UP 2001), pp. 467-68. Henry of Huntingdon, *Historica Anglorum*, edited Diana Greenway (Oxford 1996) p. 490.

66 Plutarch, *On the Intelligence of Animals*, 976a ('The Morals', Vol. V 1909).

Lampreys are soaked in their own blood for three days and served on rice. Gross, but delicious.

Some years ago, I was driven on a single track from the village of Boga over a snow-filled pass to the hamlet of Thethi (also Theth) in northern Albania close to the mountain border with Kosovo. Our vehicle was the first car of that year to make the trip. One hundred years before, traveller Edith Durham said she could think of 'no place where human beings live that has given me such an impression of majestic isolation from all the world'.[67]

Any walk around Thethi is dominated by a fortified tower, a *kullë*, where men hid for the rest of their life when their death was sought in an affair of honour or blood feud. This aspect of Albanian culture filled the mountains: there was a social obligation to kill any serious offender against the family. The practice was known as *Gjakmarrja*, 'blood-taking', and the debt extended over continuing generations. Punishment equal to the wrong done was expected under the laws of the *Kanun*, twelve books and 1,262 articles of the social code known as the 'Canon of Lekë Dukagjini'.[68]

In the steady drizzle and biting cold, I found a woman happy to prepare lunch. The painted mud walls of her log hut were pasted with old posters, peeling and torn, of long-dead heroes and singers. A trestle covered in stripped plastic cloth held two long-bubbled stews: brown bear and roe deer. Warm flat breads, part black from the outside clay oven, spilled from rough wicker baskets. There were glass jars of vicious pickles with tarnished crooked spoons ready.

I asked if the animals had been killed locally. I was told both had been shot this winter within the village fence. They had been hungry, but had stepped too far into human territory. The bear was over seven hundred kilograms, a true monster, much taller than a man, and was taken under *Kanun*.

'What has *Kanun* to do with a bear?' I asked.

'*Koka për Koke*,' she replied, a 'head for a head'. 'This *ari* killed and ate my cousin, *Lirim*. His name means "the forest".'

Here was true retaliation.

---

67 Durham, Edith, *High Albania* (Edward Arnold 1909) p. 82.
68 Kadare, Ismail, *Broken April*, (Vintage 2003) explores the social effects of an ancestral blood feud between two landowning families in Northern Albania in the 1930s. See also Kadare, *Spring Flowers, Spring Frost* (Vintage 2003).

Brown bear is second only to polar bear in size. The meat was diced and tasted of a pork venison cross, tougher and stringier than beef but with little fat, but then it had been hungry and it was killed in winter. I couldn't detect *Lirim*, but then I didn't know the extent of his contribution.

The roe deer, *kaproll*, was true venison with a slightly deeper taste as might be expected from a mountain grazer.

Two clear bottles sat on the table. One was cold hill spring water. The other was *raki thanit*, the local spirit made by fermenting the dark fruits of the wild Cornelian cherry. I found that a glass of one followed by a glass of the other, followed by … went very well.

Three other monsters, this time from the deep, seem reasonable additions to my list of animals who may have joined the retribution conspiracy: marlin, shark and swordfish. In a period when I was earning good money, I holidayed three years in a row in different West Indian islands, Antigua, Granada and Nevis. Each trip, I took one day to go deep sea fishing which I learned meant searching depths greater than thirty metres. Each new target needed an expensive specialised charter and equipment that was much cheaper to share with other hopefuls. It also meant the boat had to be robust as any catch would be distant from shore.

Each time, fish were taken. I was involved in the moment but, personally, I only caught one Atlantic blue marlin. At the end, after two long hours, even though often sitting strapped in a chair, I was worn out waiting for it to tire. I was bruised about the body with blistered hands, but elated, and then sad. The marlin is such a beautiful animal, blue above, silver beneath, with a spear on its snout and very quick in the water. My catch was just over four metres and about seven hundred kilograms.

A marlin was the centrepiece of Hemingway's classic short novel and of Forsyth's later homage, 'The Emperor'.[69]

My charter caught a three metre swordfish off Antigua. Its long, pointed, flat bill is something to see up close. While in Granada, we were supposed to be looking for another marlin, but at the end of a day filled with swells and alcohol, what we actually hooked was a bull shark. This is the one that swims up rivers and is probably responsible for most of recorded beach attacks. It is significantly bigger than a human. There were lightning fast runs, dives, surges

---

[69] Hemingway, Ernest, *The Old Man and the Sea* (1952). Forsyth, Frederick, *No Comebacks* (1982).

and crazy leaps and back flips that almost seemed impossible. This shark had an evil eye and was deemed a people attacker days before, although I never found out how it was identified. It was killed and brought aboard.

When it comes to taste, what can one say with deep sea gamefish. Shark and swordfish are often available in supermarkets. However, for me, marlin tastes like swordfish and shark is mild, meaty and slightly sweet. All three get compared to chicken, but that is one of life's go-to comparisons.

atlantic blue marlin. © NOAA.

If it's chicken you want, try alligator, the Great Retributionist. They hide, still as logs at water's edge, waiting for dangling toes on a blistering hot day or a playing child or dog. Under water, a alligator twists and turns with its prey to make drowning sure and then takes the corpse to an underwater lodge where the body is wedged and left to rot.

I shot my 'gator in the Everglades near Boca Raton in the US. I used a powered harpoon from a boat. It was pathetically easy, but a big piece of chicken.

If any animal should assume the wise leadership of a covert retribution society, it's the American bison.

European colonials were almost exclusively accountable for the near-extinction of the bison in the 1800s. An estimated fifty million were slaughtered. Railways advertised 'hunting by rail' where large herds grazed alongside or crossed tracks. Carcasses were left to rot where they fell, not even the coats taken. The excess was motivated in part by the US government's desire to limit the range and power of indigenous plains Indians whose diets and cultures depended on the herds.

One Lakota Sioux elder described the Indians' relationship with the buffalo, the American bison,

The buffalo gave us everything we needed. Without it we were nothing. Our tipis *were made of his skin. His hide was our bed, our blanket, our winter coat. It was our drum, throbbing though the night, alive, holy. Out of his skin we made our water bags. His flesh strengthened us, became flesh of our flesh. Not the smallest part of it was wasted. His stomach, a red-hot stone dropped into it, became our soup kettle. His horns were our spoons, the bones our knives, our women's awls and needles. Out of his sinews we made our bowstrings and thread. His ribs were fashioned into sleds for our children, his hoofs became rattles. His mighty skull, with the pipe leaning against it, was our sacred altar. The name of the greatest of all Sioux was Tatanka Iyotake, 'Sitting Bull'. When you killed off the buffalo you also killed the Indian, the real, natural wild Indian.*[70]

Bison were one of the very few animals I ever saw kill a human.

Bison with their shaggy coats and long hair are the largest surviving terrestrial animals in North America and Europe. They can be two metres tall and three and a half metres long. They weigh over a thousand kilograms. They are nomadic grazers and travel in herds.

female bison with young. © Dallas Penner.

---

70 Deer, John (Fire) Lame and Erdoes, Richard, *Lame Deer, Seeker of Visions* (Simon and Schuster 1972, 2009), pp. 131-32.

I was in a wildlife park in New York State watching a small group. An obese middle-aged American woman in violent pink shorts and vivid green T-shirt got out of her 4X4 to get closer to take pictures on her phone. Several signs warned her against what she was determined to do. She was shouting in her excitement and the animals were spooked and began to move away. Another large vehicle drove up quickly in their path. The bison turned and stampeded.

No matter how large the woman, she was no match for several scared bison on the run. Even my stomach turned at the mangled mess that was left after a contact lasting only a second or two. Her head was almost flat.

I ate my first bison meat that evening. I think it was the best steak I have ever had, better even than wagyu. I would choose it over beef every time. It is similar, but has a slightly sweet undertone that sets it completely apart.

I have seen both elephant and hippopotamus close up in the wild in southern Africa and eaten the meat of both, each part of a legitimate if ill-informed cull.[71]

I was beyond foolish. Driving in the Kruger Park and likely to miss the gate closure at an overnight camp, I sped around a dirt track corner. Elephant were crossing. I skidded to a halt with my bonnet just under the stomach of a large male (which was evident). As I reversed, he looked at me with the air of a disappointed teacher. He decided to let me go that time.

Hippos are the third largest land animals after rhinoceroses. I was in a small motor boat on the Kariba Dam on the Zambesi River in Zimbabwe. My teenage daughter was swimming freely a long way from shore, enticed by daredevil friends. There were crocodiles sunning on the banks as I hauled her out. A minute later a hippo broke cover and roared through its hinged and ever-widening mouth. Hippos are aggressive and unpredictable and among the most dangerous animals in the world, the careless assassins in any conspiracy.

My daughter and I had words.

One very misty early morning in a thick wood in Natal, I was surprised by a sudden crashing in the undergrowth. Six rare white rhinos intent on business and ghostly in the swirls of fog swayed by, less than five metres away, and vanished as quickly as they had appeared. My warden was so scared he dropped his .303 rifle and ran. I found him up a tree and gave him his weapon back.

---

71 Chapter, 'the great elephant cull'.

Both elephant and hippo feed mostly on vegetation and make low-carbohydrate meat, ideal for people with diabetes. The steaks are grilled or, best, charcoaled. Both are slightly gamey. My preference is most definitely for hippo, mine eaten in Zimbabwe in the Victoria Falls Hotel garden with the sound of the 'smoke that thunders' in the background. Hippo meat has about three times more unsaturated fats than beef which means that it can be cooked on a grill without any added oil.

Think of any animal retribution and it may be the larger murderers that come most easily to mind. Think longer and the really terrifying are a lot smaller.

I was in a tired taxi being driven along the straight avenue of trees that leaves the crowded temple of *Angkor Wat* on my way back to my hotel in Siem Reap for a late breakfast. I wondered if any of the endless monkeys that leapt from every nook of the site ever ended up in the long line of fast food shacks that lined both sides of the street.

I shouted at the driver. The state of the brakes didn't allow him to screech to a halt, but we did pull up eventually. Slightly set back among the banyan, palm and fig trees was something I had looked for during the last few days in Cambodia. In a small clearing with four or five close mesh cages was a shallow drum spitting with cooking oil and two small attendants in none too clean rags. The sign was in American with helpful pictures for those not in the know. Here I could buy deep-fried spiders and battered scorpions. And not just any spiders, but tree tarantulas, the ones that drop on you as you pass beneath and bite like a wasp.

Fried tarantulas, *a-ping*, became popular in the late 1970s due to food shortages during the *Khmer Rouge* regime. My tarantula was covered in a paste of caramelized sugar, salt, oil, and garlic. I pulled off a few of the legs to munch on first. It was like eating soft-shell crab. The tarantula's abdomen was gooey with a nutty taste. This is Marmite: love it or hate it. I munched the second one with a cold beer and some extra cane sugar.

Apparently, scorpions hide in every cranny of temple stones, unseen by the tourists. There are over two and a half thousand species and less than one per cent of these have venom capable of killing a human. In places where these killers do live, they murder frequently. In one country there are over two hundred thousand envenomations a year and at least three hundred deaths. If all this worries you, don't go to Mexico.

Historical scorpion motifs are everywhere, usually associated with danger or maliciousness: Islamic art, Turkish carpets, archaeology, Roman mosaics, European painting, dances, well-being postures in modern America and in the signs of the Zodiac. In Greek mythology, Artemis sent a giant scorpion to deal with the hunter Orion who had said he would kill all the world's animals. As constellations and enemies, they were placed on opposite sides of the sky so that when one rises, the other sets.

Scorpions have a surprisingly delicate blend of flavours with a slightly nutty and salty taste, similar to eating a crunchy cross between shrimp and roasted cashews. Recommended.

I have kept my worst killer till last. I say 'worst' because it almost succeeded. I am only here today because of prompt hospital treatment. You see this animal on every fishmonger's slab: the common mackerel with its tiger-like stripes and its green-blue colouring. Over five million tons are landed each year and the small fry are food for seabirds, whales, dolphins, sharks, tuna and marlin.

fried tarantula. © viajar24h.com.

Clearly there is a mackerel plan to take over the world.

Most mackerel are bottom feeders. They scrounge where the waste falls, especially near sewage pipes which makes it common off English shores. It has to be eaten on the day of capture for fear of scombroid fish poisoning. There are more references to 'stinking mackerel' in English literature than to any other fish.[72] It is well known that mackerel are unclean and feed on the flesh of dead sailors.

Here follows a warning,

> *Scombroid food poisoning, also known as simply scombroid, is a foodborne illness that typically results from eating spoiled fish. Symptoms may include flushed skin, sweating, headache, itchiness, blurred vision, abdominal cramps and diarrhoea. Onset of symptoms is typically ten to sixty minutes after eating and can last for up to two days. Rarely, breathing problems, difficulty swallowing, redness of the mouth, or an irregular heartbeat may occur. Scombroid occurs from eating fish high in histamine due to inappropriate storage or processing.*[73]

Only my attack was far worse. My face swelled to twice its size, my lips ballooned and my throat closed so much that I needed a tube to breathe. This all happened over fifty years ago in a caravan in Bude in north Cornwall. I have not eaten mackerel since.

I also know the word for mackerel in over twenty languages so that, for instance, when in Japan in a *sushi* restaurant, I can say clearly, 'No *sabu*.'

---

73 *Wikipedia* (2025).

safari biltong

impala, kangaroo, kudu, nyala, ostrich, ox, springbok, waterbuck

Biltong is a type of air-dried, cured meat originating in South Africa. The combination word is from the Afrikaans *bil,* 'buttock', and *tong* 'tongue', perhaps once a joke, now long obscured, among hardy Dutch pioneers who sought to escape would-be colonial masters. One disputed story is that in the seventeenth century large strips of raw meat were placed to dry under horses' saddles. The salty sweat preserved the meat while the constant buttock pounding tenderised it.[74]

This preservation was vital if *biltong* was to provide a reliable and rich source of protein that would keep for months and buy time while livestock herds were established. Meat can be preserved by curing it in salt, brine, malt vinegar or saltpetre, *potassium nitrate*. Saltpetre kills *clostridium botulinum*, the deadly bacterium that causes botulism, while vinegar inhibits its growth. The antimicrobial properties of some spices have been used since antiquity. For *biltong,* the Dutch majored on black pepper, salt, coriander and cloves. A 2017 Portuguese study showed that a relatively mild dose of coriander oil killed ten out of twelve strains of bacteria and significantly reduced the growth of the other two.[75]

male impala. © Charles J Sharp.

---

74 Swart, Sandra, 'Riding high – horses, power and settler society, c. 1654-1840', *Kronos*, No. 29, November 2003, pp. 47-63.

75 Silva, Filomena, 'Antimicrobial Activity of Coriander Oil and its Effectiveness as Food Preservative', *Critical Reviews in Food Science and Nutrition,* 57, 2015, pp. 35-47.

male kudu. © StormSignal.

Beef is the common constituent of today's *biltong* often from the finest cuts like fillet or sirloin. Modern seasoning has widened to include individual preferences like balsamic vinegar, brown sugar, ground chilli pepper, onion, nutmeg, paprika, lemon juice, garlic, bicarbonate of soda and Worcestershire Sauce. However, *biltong* was never intended solely for beef and included the dried meat of many other animals, for instance ostrich, chicken and a wide variety of game.

After spicing, *biltong* is air dried for at least a fortnight, often in the colder months to further inhibit bacterial and fungal growth, and then packed in ventilating cloth bags. The product is related to beef jerky, both are spiced dried meats, but the jerky is without vinegar. Jerky is also heated to at least seventy-one degrees Celsius and is often smoked. This heating encourages a faster result but, experts claim, makes an inferior end product.

Any visitor to South Africa will find *biltong* readily available in butchers' shops and in supermarkets, all with their special seasonings and unusual meats.

I first met ostrich meat as part of a breakfast on a farm in Oudtshoorn in the Western Cape. A group of four sat down to a one-egg, two-kilogram ostrich omelette, the equivalent of twenty-four brown hen's eggs. The omelette was portioned onto a thin ostrich steak: red meat, medium rare, low on fat, like veal. No one managed to empty their plate.

Later that morning, my daughter played jockey in an ostrich race over a hundred metres. These birds are the largest of the group of flightless birds: emus, rheas, cassowaries, kiwis and the extinct moas. They can reach speeds of seventy kilometres an hour. My daughter came second.

I took away with me a bag of ostrich biltong and, on an impulse, bags of ox and imported kangaroo. On the drive into Cape Town for New Year I conducted a personal and deeply scientific *biltong* experiment. All three ate very well, the ostrich like that morning's steak, the kangaroo like gamey chicken meat, high in protein and low in fat and the ox, well, just very beefy. Ox as dried meat was surpassed by a memorable meal I had in Périgueux in France during a long rugby weekend. The ox came in the form of *rognons*, 'kidneys'. I recall the food was excellent as was the wine. There was a breath-taking cheese trolley with some more wine. That's about all I can remember.

male nyala. © Charles J Sharp.

Many game animals, particularly antelopes, have been culled and *biltong* made from their meat became freely available. I can remember five other biltong purchases: impala, kudu, nyala, springbok and waterbuck, none of them seen today as threatened species.

I am hard pushed to declare any dominant taste except as game venison with kudu being the strongest flavoured. Springbok and kudu are the two prized meats and are readily available in South African supermarkets, often farmed in Namibia. Kudu flesh tastes of liver which needs to be cooked carefully to avoid it drying out. Springbok coats are also sought after and are regularly found on wall hangings and decorative products.

All of these antelopes, and many more species, are easily found in the Kruger. Impala and springbok are seemingly everywhere.

Impala are more commonly known locally as *rooibok*, 'red deer', for their coat colour. They can be found in large groups close to water and have a symbiotic relationship with oxpecker birds which is fun.

Springbok, apart from being the national symbol of South Africa and particularly of the international rugby team, are best known for their habit of pronking, multiple leaps up to two metres high in a stiff-legged posture with the back bowed. They have a distinctive black

adult springbok. © Yathin S Krishnappa.

waterbuck. © Giles Laurent.

stripe above a white belly. This antelope can live without drinking water for many years, relying on eating succulent vegetation.

Nyala and kudu males have prominent spiral horns and share vertical side stripes. The kudu's horn can be made into a musical instrument, sometimes used as a *shofar* in Yemenite Jewish ceremonies. Its hunting featured prominently in Ernest Hemingway's non-fiction book, *Green Hills of Africa*, an account of a month-long safari with his then wife Pauline Pfeiffer in East Africa in 1933.

Waterbuck also live close to water and are easily identified by the large hollow circle of white hair surrounding the tail on the rump. They give off an overwhelming smell of musk when sexually excited, noticeable even from a distance. This secretion is so unpleasant that it repels predators and gives it the nickname 'greasy kob'.

Of course, the best way to view these animals is to visit the Kruger and to stay in one of the many camps, varying from luxury tented affairs to the decidedly rustic round huts where cooking takes place outside over a log fire. Predators waiting for fresh bones circle the wire fence, usually high enough to keep them out.

sahara sickness

camel, fox, viper

Our group left Morocco astride camels and entered Mali south of Taoudenni, the hottest region on the planet, just over 400 miles and a week or so from Timbuktu. I travelled with three members of the same family: grandfather Lahcen; his son, Asso; and his grandson, Icho.[76]

Taoudenni was a feared place full of evil *djnoun* where salt was dug from the bottom of an ancient lake and cut into slabs for transportation. The managers were notorious for theft and brutality.

I fell badly ill with diarrhoea. Lahcen recognised the blackness of my discharges and was prepared for me to die. He set up camp and waited for two days while the water supplies fell dangerously low. There was only cumin for medicine which I was given freely. Mostly, I was delirious and often shouted that I was running into darkness.

Lahcen knew of an old well, perhaps five kilometres to the west and he gave Asso detailed instructions on how to find it. It would need digging out. Should it be dry, there was a second well to the north along a river bed which had not seen running water in living memory.

After two days Asso had not returned.

A first camel slumped to the ground and Lahcen stabbed the dying beast in the jugular vein at the base of the neck, drawing the blade across its throat and then went to work on the flesh - the hump, the neck, the lights, the large muscles of the thighs. Lahcen and Icho ate the jelly-like fat of the hump and the liver raw, spiced by the sour-juice from the camel's gall-bladder, the 'desert lemon'. The rest they cut into strips and hung them to dry in the thin shade of thorn-scrub. I sucked for a while on the hump-fat and liver, but soon gave up.

---

76 Heal, Chris, *Disappearing* (C&S 2019), pp. 282-285.

Camels hold water in the tissues of three stomachs, a more efficient system then storing it in the plasma of the blood as humans do. Threatened with death by thirst, we all drank the liquid from the dead camel's stomachs. As a last resort, Lahcen showed Icho how to push a stick down a camel's throat to make it vomit so that they could drink the nauseating mess.

On the third day, Icho decided to search for his father. He ignored his grandfather's objection and set off with two camels following the trail in the sand. Icho came to the dry well that his father had dug to a depth of two metres which, in the heat, would have drained him. Icho went on to the second small oasis along the long-dried river scour. Here, Asso's digging had been successful and Icho soaked his *shesh* in the water and sucked the moisture from the cloth. The camels were less fussy.

Icho found some colocynth melons growing nearby, desert succulents of the squash family with gourds as large as oranges. The pulp was bitter and started stomach-cramps. He then ate the flowers and chewed the water-filled roots. As he sat, he sling-shot a desert hare and then saw a fennec fox and dug it out of its burrow and strangled it. The animals had little meat on them, but he ate half, cooking it on stones baked in the sun and then hung the rest on the back of his saddle to dry.

Icho struck out across the plateau on a triangular path back to the camp. After a few hours, he saw circling eagles and an occasional rising vulture. He dismounted to give a break to his camel in the high sun, but kept walking through the hottest part of the day. Then he found his father's body.

Icho thought Asso had walked too close to an acacia bush and a snake had struck from its shade, without warning. The face was darkened with the poison and the skin had a yellow tinge. Icho felt for a pulse, held a mirror to his father's lips, but sensed nothing. The body was warm from the sun. To make sure, Icho found the stone black area of skin on his father's leg where the snake had struck and cut deep with his knife to

fennec fox. © Drew Avery.

that he could suck out the pus. He realised that Asso had tried to do this himself for his knife lay close to his right hand. The birds had started to peck around the eyes. It was all of no use. Asso would have taken only an hour to die, with great pain towards the end.

saharan horned viper. © Holger Krisp.

It was then that Icho saw the Torza tree, the antidote to the venom, deadly to goats. Milk-sap taken from the apple-like fruit and placed on the bite draws out the poison. Under the tree was a coiled horned viper, camouflaged by its sand-blotched skin. Icho killed it with his stick and cut off its head to take home to his mother to show that his father was avenged. He took the snake flesh to eat later and travelled with the two camels back to our camp.

Grandfather and son returned to the body where they argued whether to wash it. This the boy wanted to do, but Lahcen was worried about their water supply. They agreed to use a little water to wash the face and hands and to drystone the rest. The body was stripped of all belongings, especially the gun, knife and personal items, now Icho's property. He would take his father's turban to his mother for her memory and so that, in the deep of the night, she could take it from under her pillow and smell it and bring her husband back to her. A grave was dug facing sunrise deep enough for a half metre covering. Pointed stones were placed over the head and the feet so that those who followed would know that a devout Berber's body lay there who was deserving of respect.

The grandfather and the grandson prayed together and then silently rose and rode back. Lahcen was a broken man. I was severely dehydrated, but lucid enough to hear the news.

'I want to give you freedom from your promise to me to take me to Timbuktu,' I said. 'I am going to die anyway. You have the suffered a deep loss. If you feel that it is right to return home then I support your decision.'

'My father is with Allah,' Icho replied, 'and he watches over us. Inshallah, we will reach Timbuktu even though you may die on the way. My grandfather welcomes the respect in your offer. However, I have no choice but to complete my father's contract with you. And, even if I did have a choice, I would do no different. We are bound together.'

Nothing more was said. Just as the sun first cracked across the horizon, I was tied to my saddle and given pieces of sun-dried viper and fox to chew.

They tasted of nothing at all.

*As firmly-cemented clam-shells
Fall apart in autumn,
So I must take to the road again,
Farewell, my friends.*[77]

---

77 Bashō, Matsuo, *The Narrow Road to the Deep North* (Penguin 1966; 1694), p. 142.

full list with place(s) of best meal (150)

1	Abalone	Gisborne, New Zealand
2	Alligator	Boca Raton, USA
3	Anchovy	Nice, France
4	Ant, Weaver	Sipandon, Laos
5	Armadillo	Tobago, West Indies
6	Barnacle	Largs, Scotland
7	Bear	Thethi, Albania
8	Bison	New York State, USA
9	Boar	Durbuy, Belgium
10	Brill	Petersfield, England
11	Bug, stink	Sipandon, Laos
12	Butterfish	Walvis Bay, Namibia
13	Camel	Taoudenni, Mali
14	Carp	Tsumago, Japan
15	Catfish, channel	Boca Raton, USA
16	Chicken	Landi Kotal, Pakistan
17	Clam	Ravello and Tremezzo, Italy
18	Cockle	Southend, England
19	Cockroach	Mirjaveh, Iran
20	Cod	Uli, Biafra; Faro, Portugal
21	Coley	London
22	Conch	Antigua, West Indies
23	Conger eel	Largs, Scotland
24	Cow	Takayama, Japan
25	Crab	Durban, South Africa
26	Crawfish	Angle, Wales
27	Crayfish, signal	Hay-on-Wye, Wales
28	Crevette	Johannesburg; Normandy, France
29	Cricket, house	Sipandon, Laos

30	Cricket, short-tailed	Sipandon, Laos
31	Crocodile	Niamey, Niger; Can Tho, Vietnam
32	Crow	Delhi
33	Cuttlefish	Rethymno, Crete
34	Dab	Falmouth, England
35	Dog	Hue, Vietnam
36	Dormouse	Jerusalem
37	Duck, Aylesbury	Petersfield, England
38	Duck, Eider	Hay-on-Wye, Wales
39	Eel	Southend, England
40	Elephant	Kruger Park, South Africa
41	Fox, fennec	Taoudenni, Mali
42	Frog	Lyon, France
43	Gannet	Skye, Scotland
44	Goat	Kandahar, Afghanistan
45	Goose	Budapest; Normandy, France
46	Grasshopper	Sipandon, Laos
47	Grouper	Bodrum, Turkey
48	Gurnard	Auckland, New Zealand
49	Haddock	Four Marks, England
50	Hake	Johannesburg
51	Halibut	New York
52	Hippopotamus	Victoria Falls, Zimbabwe
53	Horse	Paris
54	Horse mussel	Lochgilphead, Scotland
55	Impala	Kruger Park, South Africa
56	Kangaroo	Auckland, New Zealand
57	Kingklip	Johannesburg
58	Kipper	Mull, Scotland
59	Krill	Normandy, France
60	Kudu	Kruger Park, South Africa
61	Lamprey	Montemor-o-Velho, Portugal
62	Langoustine	Normandy, France
63	Lobster	Little Cumbrae, Scotland
64	Lumpfish	Four Marks, England
65	Mackerel	Bude, England

full list with place(s) of best meal (150)

66	Mahi-mahi	Seychelles, Indian Ocean
67	Marlin	Nevis, West Indies
68	Monkey	Brazzaville, Congo
69	Monkfish	Petersfield, England
70	Mussel	Ghent, Belgium
71	Nile perch	Upper Egypt
72	Nile tilapia	Upper Egypt
73	Nyala	Kruger Park, South Africa
74	Octopus	Thessalonica, Greece
75	Ostrich	Oudtshoorn, South Africa
76	Ox	Périgueux, France
77	Oyster	Galway, Eire; Paris; Concale, France
78	Partridge	Four Marks, England
79	Penguin, Emperor	Paradise Bay, Antarctica
80	Periwinkle	Normandy, France
81	Pheasant	Four Marks, England
82	Pig	Avellino, Italy; West Bromwich, England
83	Pike	Hay-on-Wye, Wales
84	Plaice	Dover, England
85	Pollock	London
86	Prawn	Normandy, France
87	Python, rock	Niamey, Niger
88	Quail	Four Marks, England
89	Queenie scallop	Largs, Scotland
90	Rabbit	Gozo, Malta
91	Rabbitfish	Seychelles, Indian Ocean
92	Razor fish	Caernarvon, Wales
93	Red deer	Four Marks, England
94	Red mullet	Petersfield, England
95	Ricefield rat	Vang Vieng, Laos
96	Roach	Hay-on-Wye, Wales
97	Roe deer	Thethi, Albania
98	Salmon	Edinburgh
99	Sandre	Saumur, Loire Valley
100	Sardine	Albufeira, Portugal
101	Scallop	Summer Isles, Scotland

102	Scorpion	Siem Reap, Cambodia
103	Seabass	Tunis
104	Seabream	Ascension Island, Atlantic Ocean
105	Seal	Paradise Bay, Antarctica
106	Sea urchin	Campbeltown, Scotland
107	Sewin	Fishguard, Wales
108	Shark	Granada, West Indies
109	Sheep	Quetta, Pakistan
111	Shrimp	Southport, England
111	Sild	Petersfield, England
112	Skate	Great Cumbrae, Scotland
113	Snail	Lyon, France
114	Snapper, red	Nevis, West Indies
115	Snipe	Aldeburgh, England
116	Snoek	Johannesburg
117	Sole, Dover	Petersfield, England
118	Spider crab	Concale, France
119	Spiny dogfish	London
120	Sprat	Petersfield, England
121	Springbok	Kruger Park, South Africa
122	Squid	Rome
123	Squirrel	New York State, USA
124	Sturgeon	London
125	Swan	London
126	Swordfish	Antigua, West Indies
127	Tarantula	Siem Reap, Cambodia
128	Tench	Hay-on-Wye, Wales
129	Tilapia	New York
130	Trout, rainbow	Petersfield, England
131	Trout, brown	Skelmorlie, Scotland
132	Tuna, bigeye	Grande Comore, Indian Ocean
133	Tuna, bluefin	Tokyo
134	Tuna, yellowfin	London
135	Turbot	Porthleven, England
136	Turkey	Four Marks, England
137	Turtle	Tangalle, Sri Lanka

138	Unknown fish	Seychelles, Indian Ocean
139	Viper	Taoudenni, Mali
140	Walrus	Paradise Bay, Antarctica
141	Wasp	Sipandon, Laos
142	Warthog	Tswalu, South Africa
143	Waterbuck	Kruger Park, South Africa
144	Weevil, palm	Sipandon, Laos
145	Whale, killer	Paradise Bay, Antarctica
146	Whale, minke	Tokyo
147	Whelk	Normandy, France
148	Whitebait	Petersfield, England
149	Whiting	London
150	Wood pigeon	Four Marks, England

Chris Heal's books are available through major internet booksellers. Find details at www.candspublishing.org.uk where most can also be bought.

Sound of Hunger (2018)

An acclaimed social biography of two brothers, Erich and Georg Gerth, WW1 u-boat captains, set against Germany's political and militaristic development from Bismarck to Hitler. A fast-paced, true detective story that tracks across archives, places and events in Europe and Africa. A selected book in several German universities for its surprising English perspective.

Disappearing (2019) (first part of semi-autobiography)

A nomad with a violent past, infuriated by petty bureaucracy and the surveillance society, determines to live happily ever after, throwing off identity and leaving no trace. Things go awry: fighting for Biafran secessionists, gun running in Morocco, murder in Brussels, terrorists in Nairobi and a deathly Saharan escape. Semi-autobiographical.

Reappearing (2020) (second and concluding part of semi-autobiography)

The sequel to Disappearing. *If an elderly couple save you from a bad death in the Sahara, there's an honest debt to be paid. But this couple have conflicting plans. The only escape is down the River Niger where some unpleasant people await. The hunt is on for an elusive father who fought for the French across the globe in the dog days of empire.*

The Four Marks Murders (2020) *(first part of the Ridge Trilogy)*

In this true-life thriller, Chris Heal investigates deliberate and untimely deaths in what was thought to be one of the quiet backwaters of Hampshire. The twenty murders begin in Roman times with over half since 1900 and three within the last few years. They beg the question, 'Is Four Marks the murder capital of Southern England?'

Ropley's Legacy (2021) *(second part of the Ridge Trilogy)*

The Ridge Enclosures, 1709 to 1850: Chawton, Farringdon, Medstead, Newton Valence and Ropley and the birth of Four Marks.

The first private parliamentary enclosure in England was in 1709 in Ropley. Driven by the less than saintly bishop of Winchester, it was a highly contested land grab seeking to make money by taking control of the common fields. Over 150 years, the government sanctioned theft spread to all the neighbouring ridge villages. A detailed history.

The Winchester Tales (2022) *(concluding part of the Ridge Trilogy)*

An Anglo-Norman love story set during the invasion of England after 1066.

Gilbert of Bayeux, orphan, linguist and administrator, is brought to Winchester by Bishop Odo in 1067 to mastermind the appropriation of the land of the Saxon thegns fallen at Hastings. For the next forty years, he treads a precarious path through the Norman occupation. His great love, Ailgifu, is an outspoken mead seller from Medstead. His servant, Lēofric, provides challenging and dangerous company.

Bad Moon Rising (2023)

Three disturbing short stories about despair.

Disgraced soldier Billy Budd returns to Alton in Hampshire having lost all belief in authority. His great wish is to destroy those who make the rules. Mary May is a recently widowed pensioner without family or close friends. Much of the overworked welfare community has retreated behind websites. The Russians deploy nuclear weapons in Ukraine to disastrous effect. Two survivors aboard the international space station are flung into the great void.

The War of the Raven (2023)

The career of Kapitänleutnant Georg Gerth 1888-1970.

Georg Gerth volunteered for u-boat command to counter England's attempt to starve Germany into submission. His patrols took him into the North Sea, the English Channel and the French Atlantic. Stranded south of Calais, his boat proved a trove of intelligence. He was imprisoned, tried to escape, but was incarcerated as a pawn until the Versailles Treaty. His story is backed by extensive research and private interviews with his descendants.

Saints & Sinners (2023)

The career of Kapitänleutnant Erich Gerth 1886-1943.

Between the world wars, three powerful men befriended the young u-boat captain, Erich Gerth, all vehemently anti-communist and on the far right of German politics: master spy Wilhelm Canaris, Admiral Adolf von Trotha and 'Consul' Salomon Marx, Jewish powerbroker. Gerth's career and life was doomed by his marriage to a young widow, Gräfin Eva von Ahlefeldt. The story is backed by extensive research and private interviews with his family.

La dernière patrouille de l'UC 61 (2023) with Henri Lesoin

A French view of the last patrol of Georg Gerth's u-boat, UC 61.

The story, based largely on Chris Heal's books, Sound of Hunger *and* The War of the Raven, *has been translated into French and updated by Lt. Col. Henri Lesoin and his naval and community colleagues in Wissant, the site of the boat's stranding. Lesoin has introduced many additional photographs and insights.*

Glimpses of the Famous (2025)

Seventy brief and personal conversations

Lying in a hospital bed after a heart attack, Chris Heal retreats from the noise of the ward. He plays a private counting game, 'How many famous people has he met?' This book is the result: short stories about seventy famous people, all personal moments, mostly fleeting, always as truthful as memory allows, with humour and with no punches pulled.

www.ingramcontent.com/pod-product-compliance
Lightning Source LLC
Chambersburg PA
CBHW061231070526
44584CB00030B/4079